Mandolin Picking Tunes
EARLY MUSIC GEMS

by Dix Bruce

www.melbay.com/30818MEB

Special thanks to Kathi Bruce for her suggestions and photography.

© 2020 by Mel Bay Publications, Inc. All Rights Reserved.
WWW.MELBAY.COM

Table of Contents

Title	Page	Audio
Andante Lute	9	1
Branle Double	10	2
Greensleeves	12	3
Gavotte	15	4
Saltarello	16	5
Kemp's Jig	18	6
Canarios	20	7
Ballade Lute	23	8
Wilson's Wilde	24	9
The Bear Dance	25	10
Spagnoletta	26	11
Guardeme las Vacas	28	12
Adoro Devote	31	13
Alman	32	14
La Folias	34	15
To Drive the Cold Winter Away	36	16
Pastourelle	38	17

Title	Page	Audio
Childgrove	40	18
Allegro Lute	42	19
St. Martins	43	20
Moderato Lute	44	21
Come with Me, My Giselle	46	22
O Esca Viatorum	48	23
Volte	50	24
Tutte Venite Armati	51	25
Grimstock	52	26
Dont vient cela	54	27
Fortune My Foe	56	28
An Italian Rant	58	29
On the Cold Ground	59	30
Rendez Á Dieu	60	31
Si Pour t'Aymer	62	32
Packington's Pound	64	33
Chestnut	66	34

About the Author

Dix Bruce is a musician and writer from the San Francisco Bay Area. He has authored over fifty books, recordings, and videos for Mel Bay Publications. All are available from his website: musixnow.com. Dix performs and does studio work on guitar, mandolin, bass, and banjo. He has recorded two albums with mandolin legend **Frank Wakefield**; eight big band CDs with the **Royal Society Jazz Orchestra**; his own collection of American folk songs entitled *My Folk Heart* on which he plays guitar, mandolin, autoharp and sings; and a CD of string swing and jazz entitled *Tuxedo Blues*. He has released four CDs of traditional American songs and originals with guitarist **Jim Nunally**, including a collection of "brother duet" style recordings entitled *Brothers at Heart*. His CD with singer and mandolinist **Julie Cline** is entitled *Look at it Rain*. *Brothers at Heart* and *Look at it Rain* are available from iTunes, CDBaby, and from Dix's website. Dix also arranged, composed, and played mandolin on the sound tracks to four different editions of the best-selling computer game *The Sims*.

Also by Dix Bruce:

Wedding Music for Mandolin book/audio set – includes 23 of the most popular and best-loved wedding hits for intermediate and advanced mandolinists.

Mandolin Licks-ercises, DVD and streaming – video licks, tunes, and exercises for beginning and intermediate players.

The Parking Lot Picker's Songbooks – six separate book/audio sets for mandolin, guitar, banjo, fiddle, resonator guitar, and bass. (Mel Bay)

Parking Lot Picker's Play-Along: Mandolin, book/audio set – 15 all-time great bluegrass, old time, and gospel hits recorded in play-along style. (Mel Bay)

Bluegrass Breaks: Mandolin – For beginning and intermediate mandolinists, this book contains a collection of various mandolin solos in a range of styles and levels of difficulty. (Mel Bay)

Gypsy Swing & Hot Club Rhythm for Mandolin, Vol. I & II book/audio sets. (Musix)

Gypsy Swing & Hot Club Rhythm for Guitar, Vol. I & II, book/audio sets. (Musix)

All-Time Favorite Parking Lot Picker's Mandolin Solos, book/audio set. (Mel Bay)

All-Time Favorite Parking Lot Picker's Guitar Solos, book/audio set. (Mel Bay)

Christmas Favorites for Solo Guitar (30 Best Loved Traditional Songs for Bluegrass Guitar), book/audio set. (Mel Bay)

You Can Teach Yourself Mandolin, book/audio/video set. (Mel Bay)

Favorite Mandolin Picking Tunes, book/audio set. (Mel Bay)

Mandolin Uff Da! Let's Dance: Scandinavian Fiddle Tunes & House Party Music, book/audio set. (Mel Bay)

Dix Bruce's Swing & Jazz Mandolin DVD: Chords, Rhythm, and Songs. DVD that teaches everything you need to know to get up and swinging on the mandolin! (Musix)

Getting into Bluegrass Mandolin, book/audio set. (Mel Bay)

First Lessons: Mandolin, book/audio set. (Mel Bay)

Mandolin Picking Tunes:
Early Music Gems
by Dix Bruce

A life in music is a journey of discovery. There's always a new technique, chord, lick, song, style, or historical period to explore. Discovering new music is a joy. The music in this book will be new to many of you, but any efforts you make to explore it will be richly rewarded. It's beautiful music and fun to play!

That said, this music is anything but "new." Most of it has been around for four to eight hundred years. It's often referred to as "ancient music" or "early music" – hence our title "Early Music Gems." Many of the pieces in this book, mostly composed between the 1200s and 1600s, are part of the classical guitar repertoire, and it turns out that they make very nice mandolin tunes. Depending upon your level on the mandolin, some of them might be very challenging. But don't let that deter you! All are playable with some study and practice.

In writing these mandolin arrangements I often simplified the original music. I started by limiting the number of chord strums in a piece. I also adjusted the octaves of passages to better accommodate the range of the mandolin and, in some cases, to simplify the performance. I aimed the arrangements at intermediate and advanced players.

Often the standard notation of songs like these is written in two voices. If you're not used to reading two parts, the standard notation can be daunting. It looks like this:

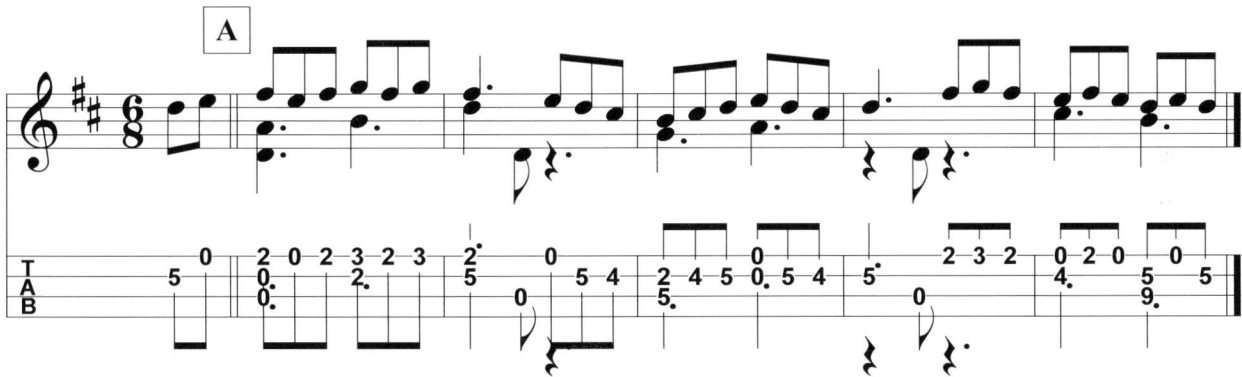

I combined the voices and wrote these arrangements as one part. Hopefully this method will make the reading a little easier, especially for those of you who are unused to reading standard notation.

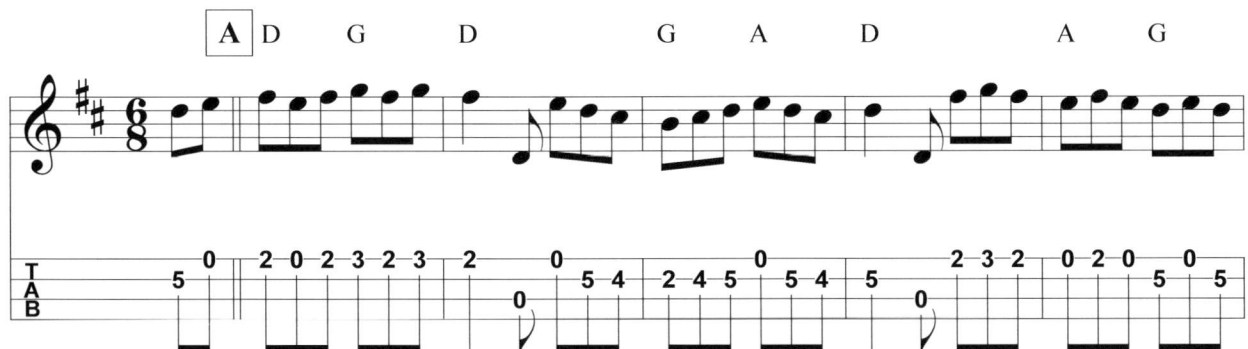

Technically speaking the most challenging aspect of the music is to smoothly integrate chord strums with single note playing. The trick is to play a good clean chord and let it ring until you play the following notes. Try to have the chord strums fit dynamically with the surrounding notes. Don't let the strums pop out too much.

The tablature or TAB line is located under the standard notation. I added circles and ovals to the tablature to represent half or longer notes. Here's an excerpt:

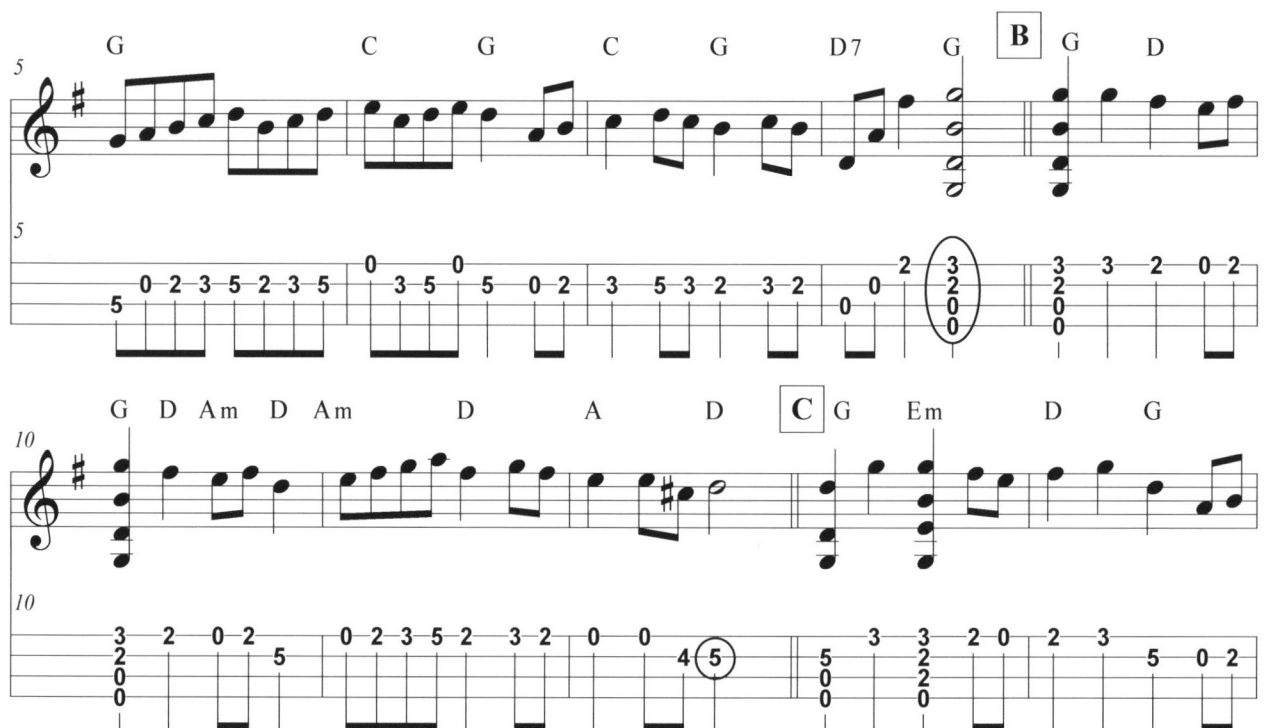

A single TAB number with a circle plus a stem indicates a half note. Ovals on more than one stacked TAB number indicate strums across more than one string. A circle without a stem indicates a whole note. Dots after circles or ovals work just like dots in standard notation and add half of a note's value to it. If a half note gets two beats, a dotted half gets three.

These arrangements can be played as mandolin solos but I also included accompaniment chords in the music so that you can perform these songs in ensembles with chordal instruments. The rudimentary guitar accompaniment on the recordings will give you a chordal background to play along with. The recorded guitar parts are quite simple and sometimes consist of just one or two chord strums per measure. Encourage your accompanist to augment the parts as they see fit no matter what instrument they play.

All of the songs have been recorded and are downloadable. (See the link on the title page.) By adjusting the balance of your playback device, you can hear just mandolin (right channel), just guitar accompaniment (left channel), or both by listening in stereo. If you're listening on headphones you can take one or the other side away from your ear to get a similar effect. As I'm writing this software called "Audacity" is available that allows you to import audio and control the pan of the playback through your computer or smart phone.

If these recordings are too fast for you to play along with, use "The Amazing SlowDowner" or similar software to slow them down. I also suggest that you practice each song with a metronome at slower tempos before you attempt to play along with the recording. First sight read through a piece a few times without it, then set the metronome at a speed slow enough to play it top to bottom without stopping and restarting. Set this slow speed at the tempo you can successfully play the most difficult passage. As you work on a song gradually increase the metronome speed to approach the target tempo shown at the upper left of the first page of each piece. These are only suggested tempos. If you feel the song faster or slower, play it as you wish!

These songs come from a very different era than our current one. Compared to the pop, folk, rock, and country songs of the last hundred and fifty years, many have unusual chords and chord progressions. At first I found some of them a little jarring but after a bit of study I began to see how they worked. Check out "Spagnoletta" (page 26) for an example of unusual chord juxtapositions.

Some of the songs include time signatures other than 4/4 and 3/4. 6/8 is quite prevalent as is 6/4 and 2/4. Some songs change from one meter to another. "O Esca Viatorum" (page 48) mixes 4/4 and 3/2. "Rendez Á Dieu" (page 60) combines 4/4 and 6/4. If you're not used to performing these meter changes, slow everything down and play along with a metronome. Count the notes with the metronome and try singing them. Don't worry about the pitches – concentrate on singing the timing of the notes. These meter changes can seem like puzzles at first, but I know you'll have a great feeling of accomplishment once you solve them.

In addition to unusual chords, progressions, and meter combinations, you may run across some unusual rhythmic combinations that you'll need to practice in advance. I'm thinking of songs like "On the Cold Ground" (page 59) where you'll find yourself playing consecutive dotted 1/8-1/16-1/8 note combinations followed by three 1/8 notes. Here's an excerpt:

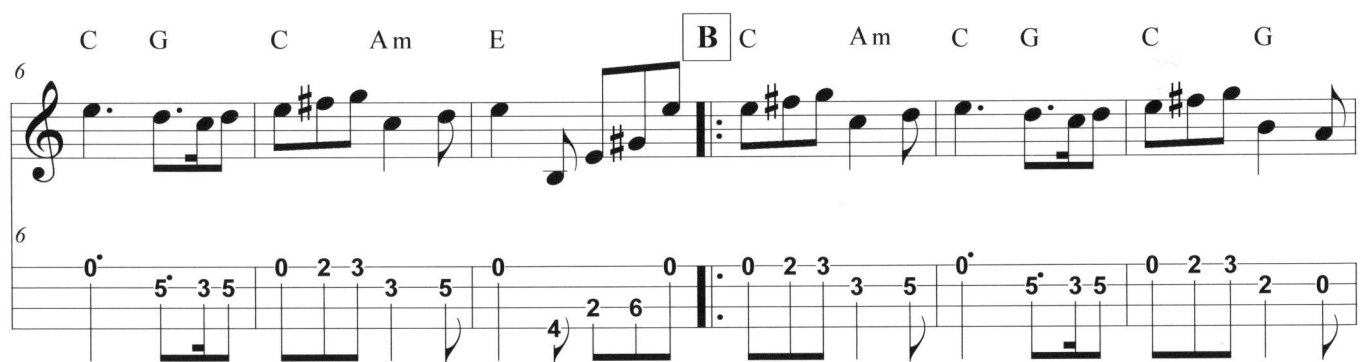

If certain rhythms have you stumped, consult the downloadable recordings and play along.

Some of the songs have passages with big note leaps on the fingerboard. I added a very few fretting finger suggestions to help out. You should be able to figure out logical fingerings elsewhere.

Some of the pieces are quite short. I suggest that in performance you consider playing parts or whole pieces through more than once or combine two or more pieces into a medley.

Composers and composition dates are given if known.

All of these pieces are wonderful, but I have some special favorites. I know you'll enjoy "Branle Double" (page 10), "Kemp's Jig" (page 18), "Canarios" (page 20), "Wilson's Wilde" (page 24) and "Grimstock" (page 52). I'm sure you're familiar with the song "Greensleeves" (page 12). This arrangement unfolds with variations on the basic theme, and audiences will love it because it's so familiar and easy to follow.

I hope you'll check out my other mandolin books and videos. (See page 4.) The most recent is "Wedding Music for Mandolin." It contains traditional wedding melodies, many of which are based on classical compositions more recent than these early music pieces.

Special thanks to Bill Bay for introducing me to this great music and for allowing me to use his guitar arrangements as a basis for my mandolin arrangements.

As I mentioned above, working on these arrangements has been a rewarding journey of discovery for me. I'm happy that you could share that journey with me and hope that you find this early music enriching and worthwhile.

Dix Bruce
Summer 2020

Dix Bruce

Andante Lute

Andante ♩ = 86

Anonymous
Arr. by Dix Bruce

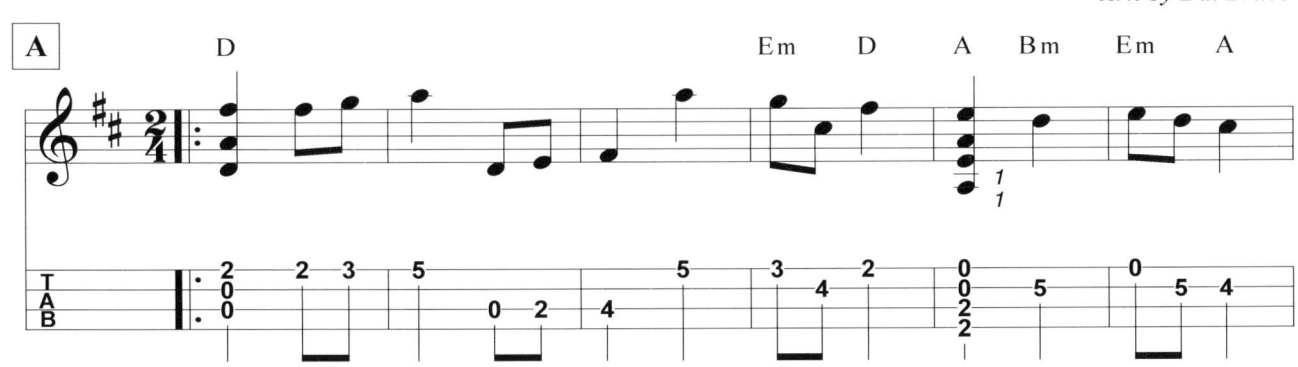
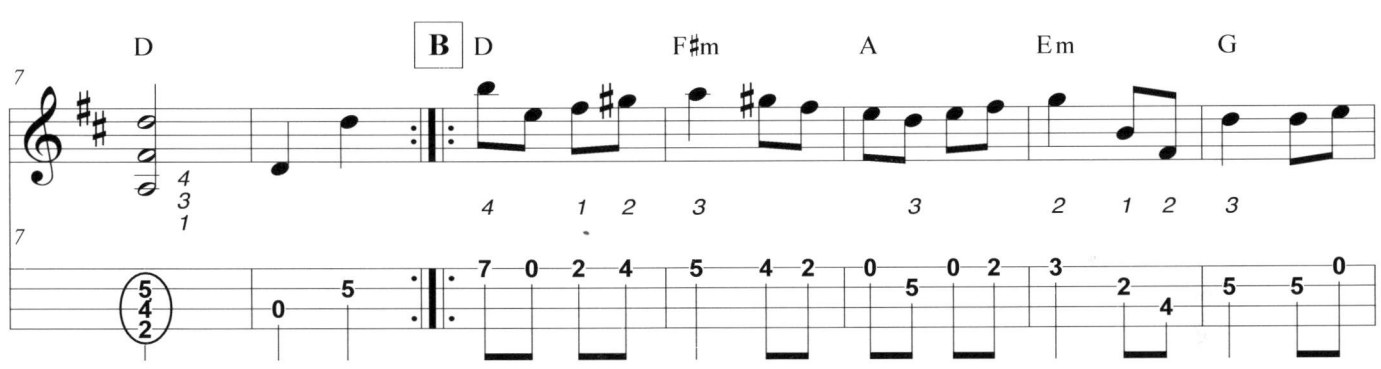
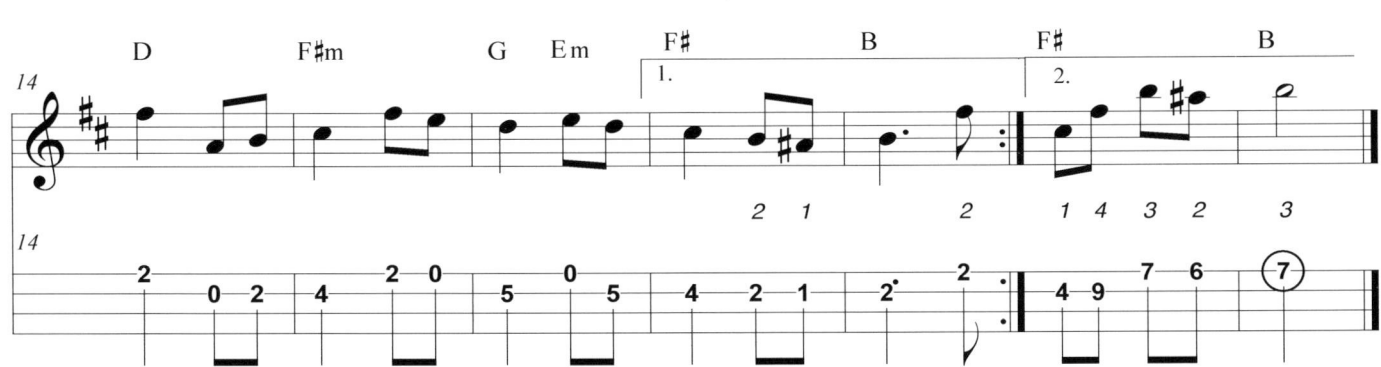

Branle Double

Moderato ♩ = 138

Michael Praetorious
Arr. by Dix Bruce

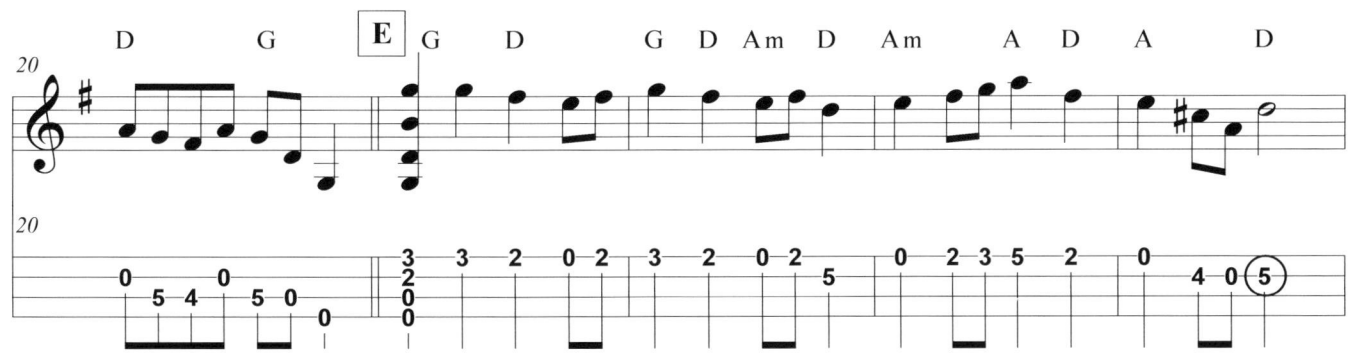
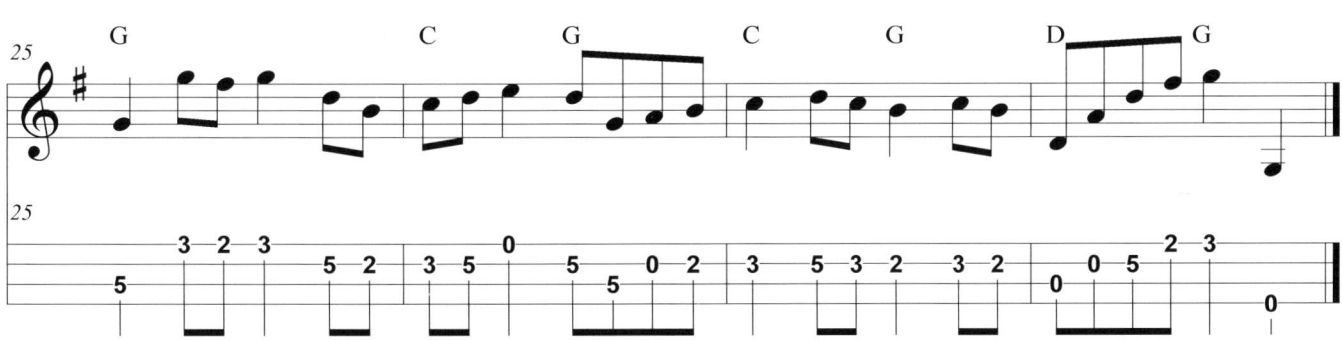

Greensleeves

Anonymous
Arr. by Dix Bruce

Allegro ♩ = 115

Gavotte

Allegro ♩ = 126

Michael Praetorius
Arr. by Dix Bruce

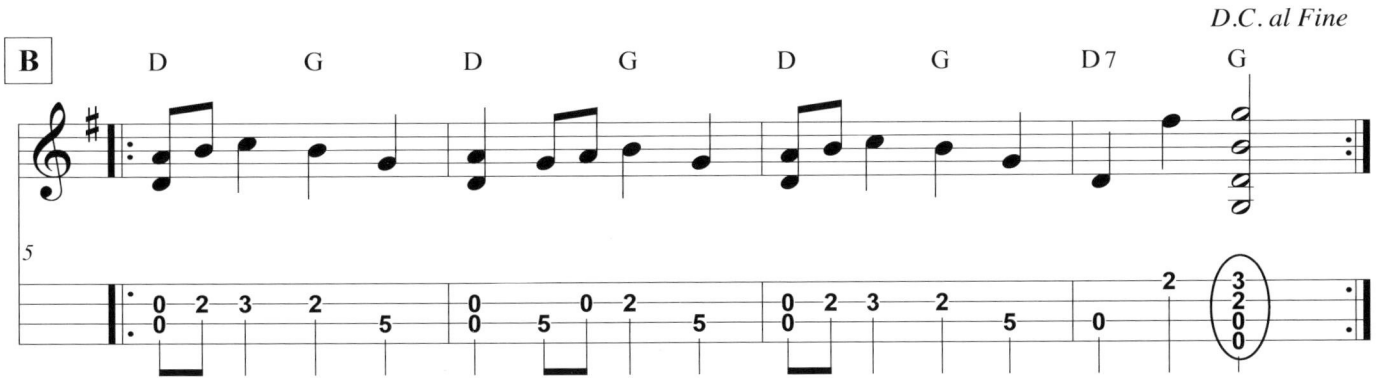

15

Saltarello

Vincenzo Galilei
Arr. by Dix Bruce

Allegro ♩ = 130

Kemp's Jig

Stately ♩ = 82

John Playford
Arr. by Dix Bruce

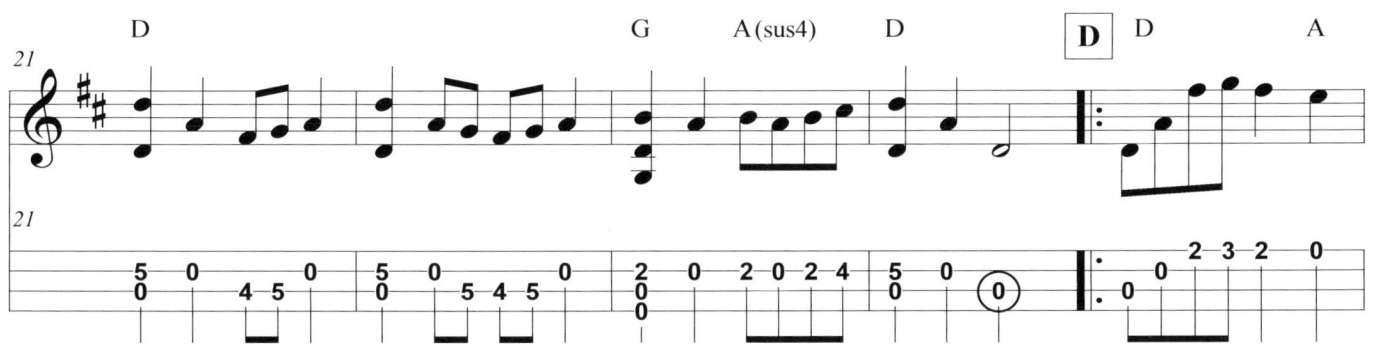
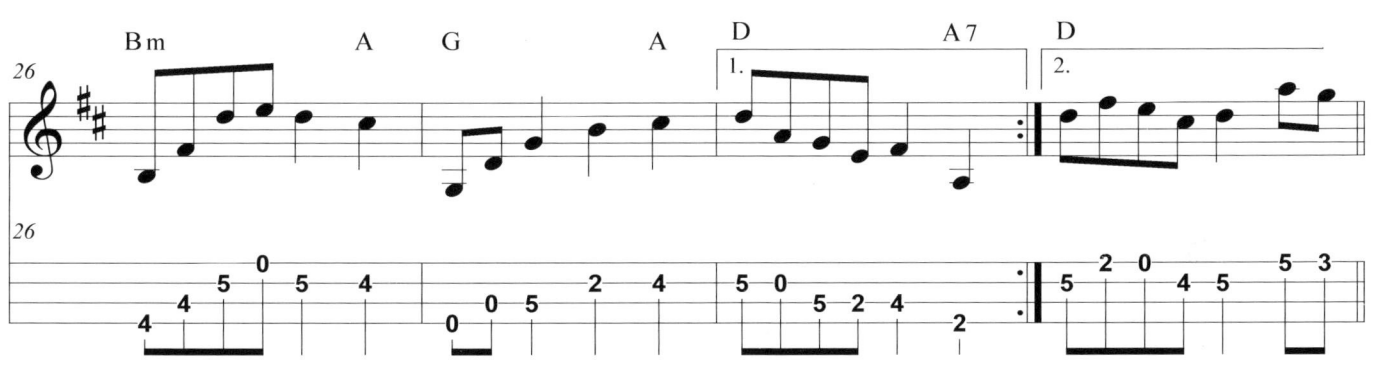
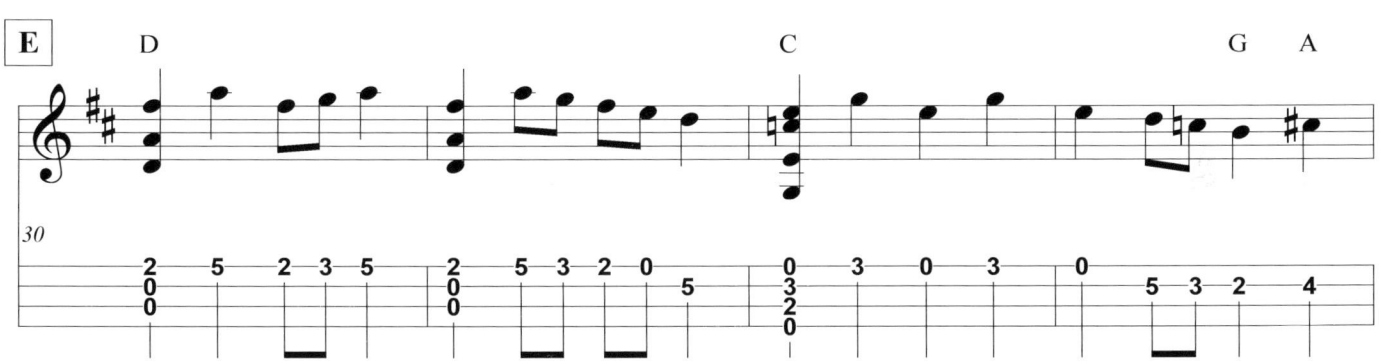
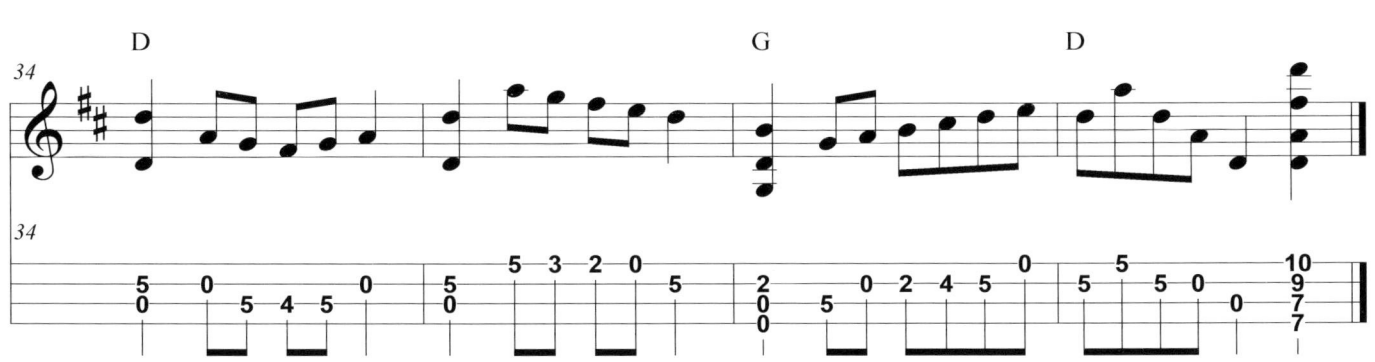

Canarios

Allegro ♩. = 84

Gaspar Sanz
Arr. by Dix Bruce

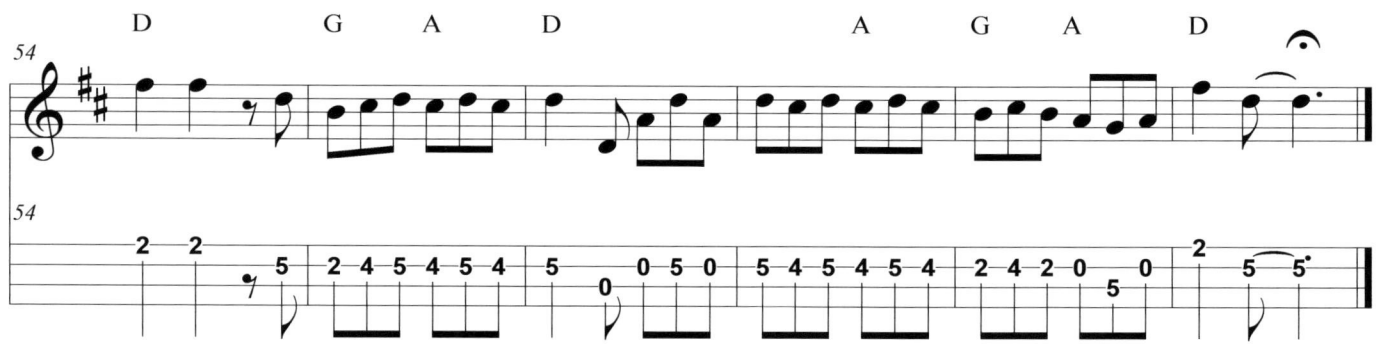

Ballade Lute

Unknown
Arr. by Dix Bruce

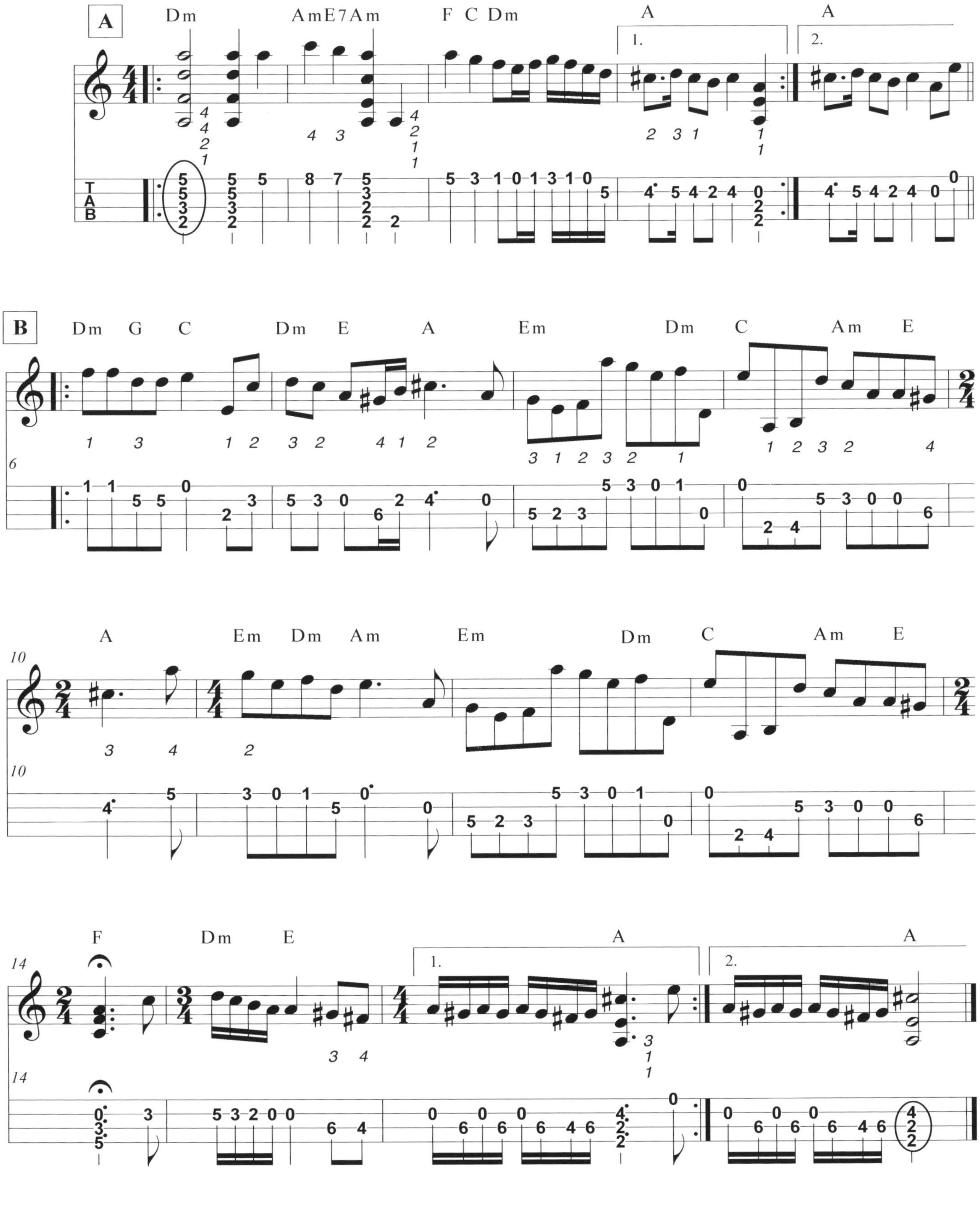

Adagio ♩ = 68

Wilson's Wilde

Allegro ♩. = 55

Attributed to John Dowland
Arr. by Dix Bruce

The Bear Dance

Unknown
Arr. by Dix Bruce

Lively ♩ = 98

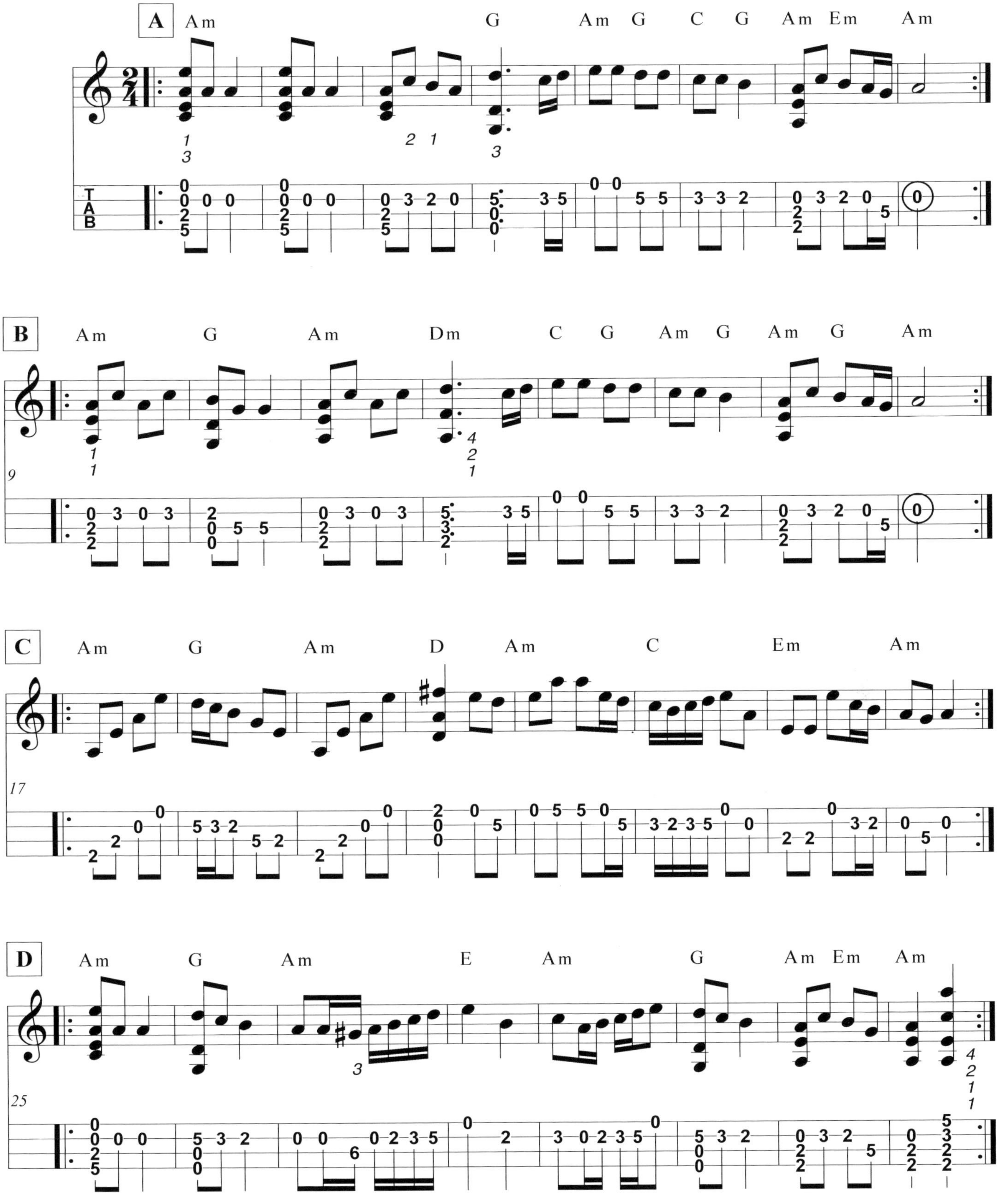

Spagnoletta

Moderato ♩ = 144

Michael Praetorious
Arr. by Dix Bruce

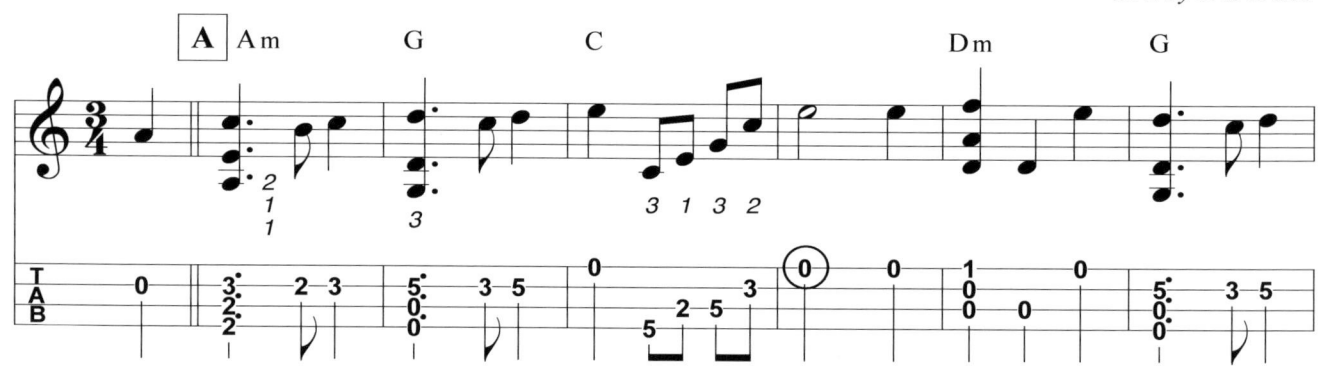
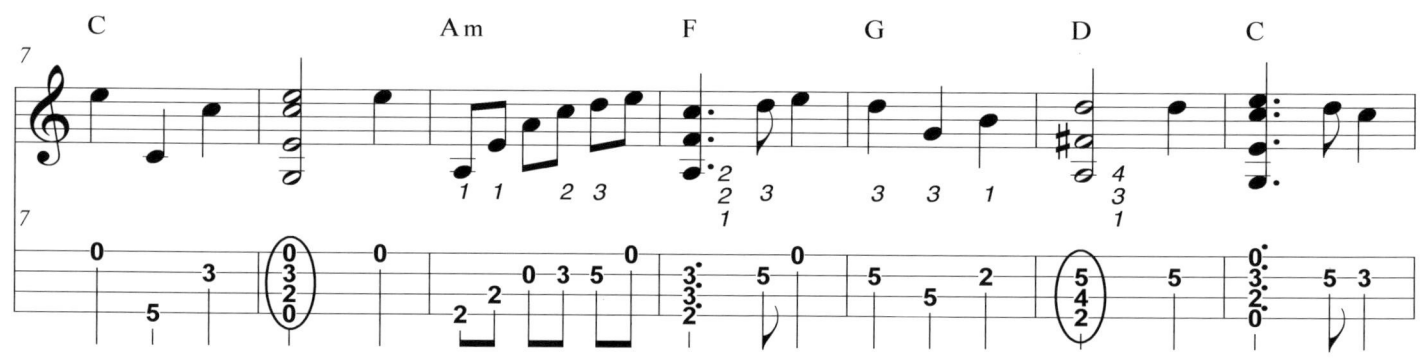
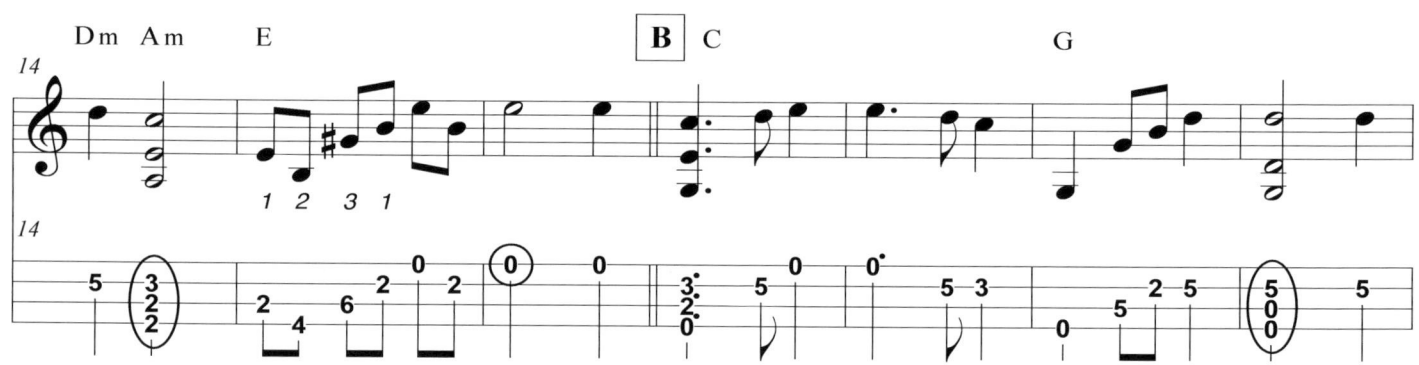
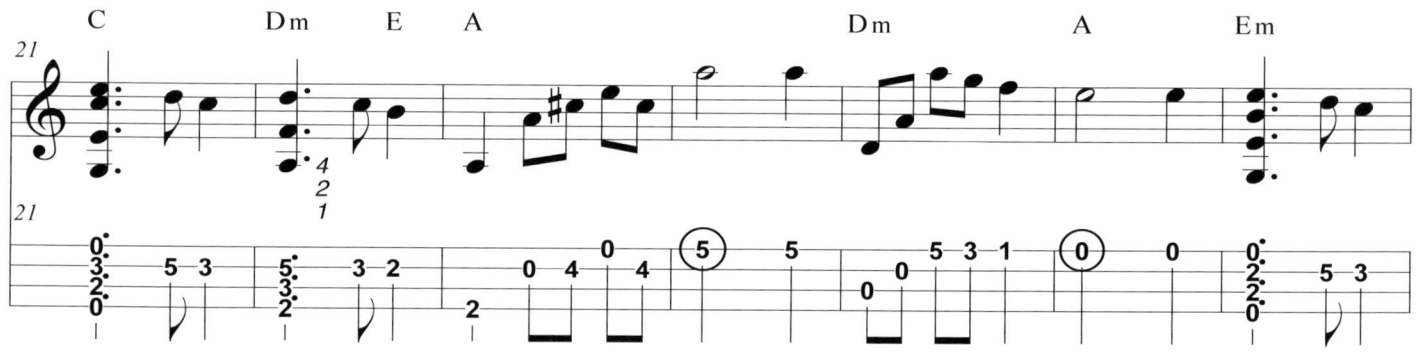

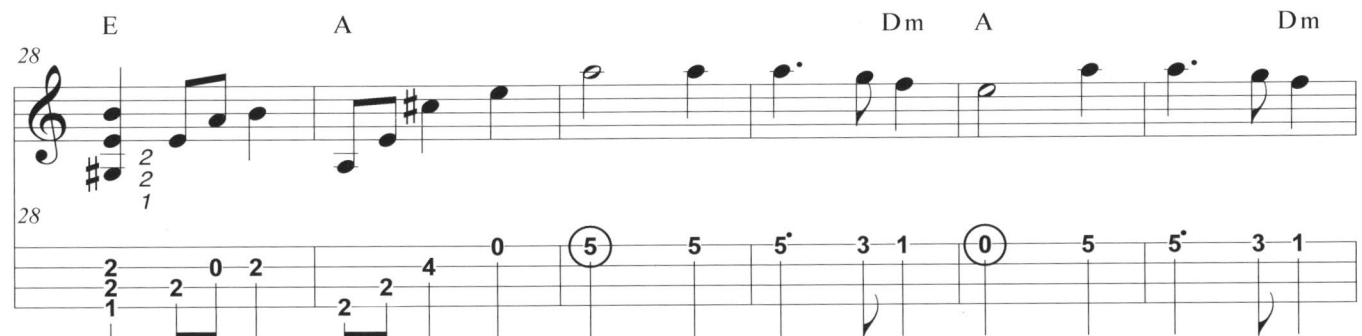
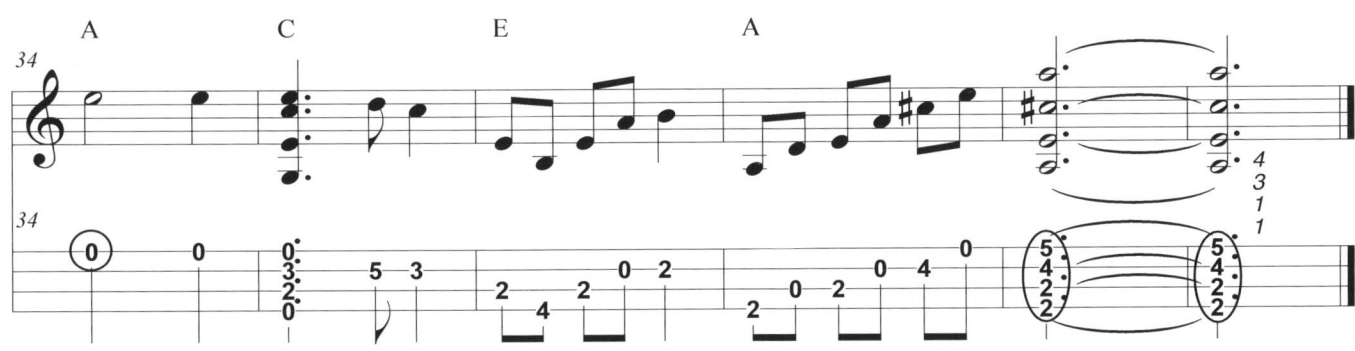

Guardeme las Vacas

Luis de Narvaez
Arr. by Dix Bruce

Allegro ♩ = 110

Adoro Devote

13th Century Plainsong
Arr. by Dix Bruce

Moderately Slow ♩ = 64

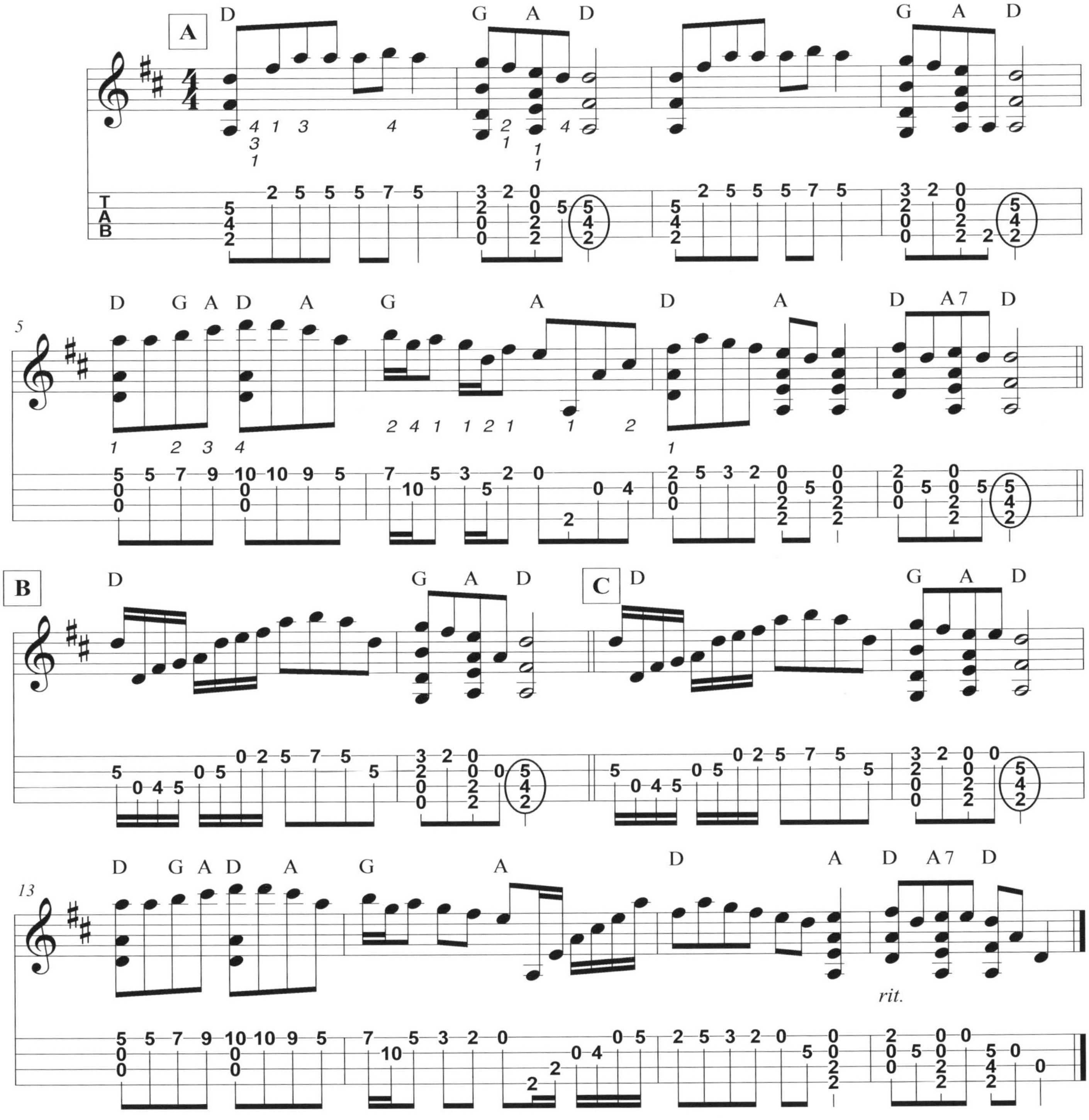

Alman

Moderato ♩=96

Robert Johnson
Arr. by Dix Bruce

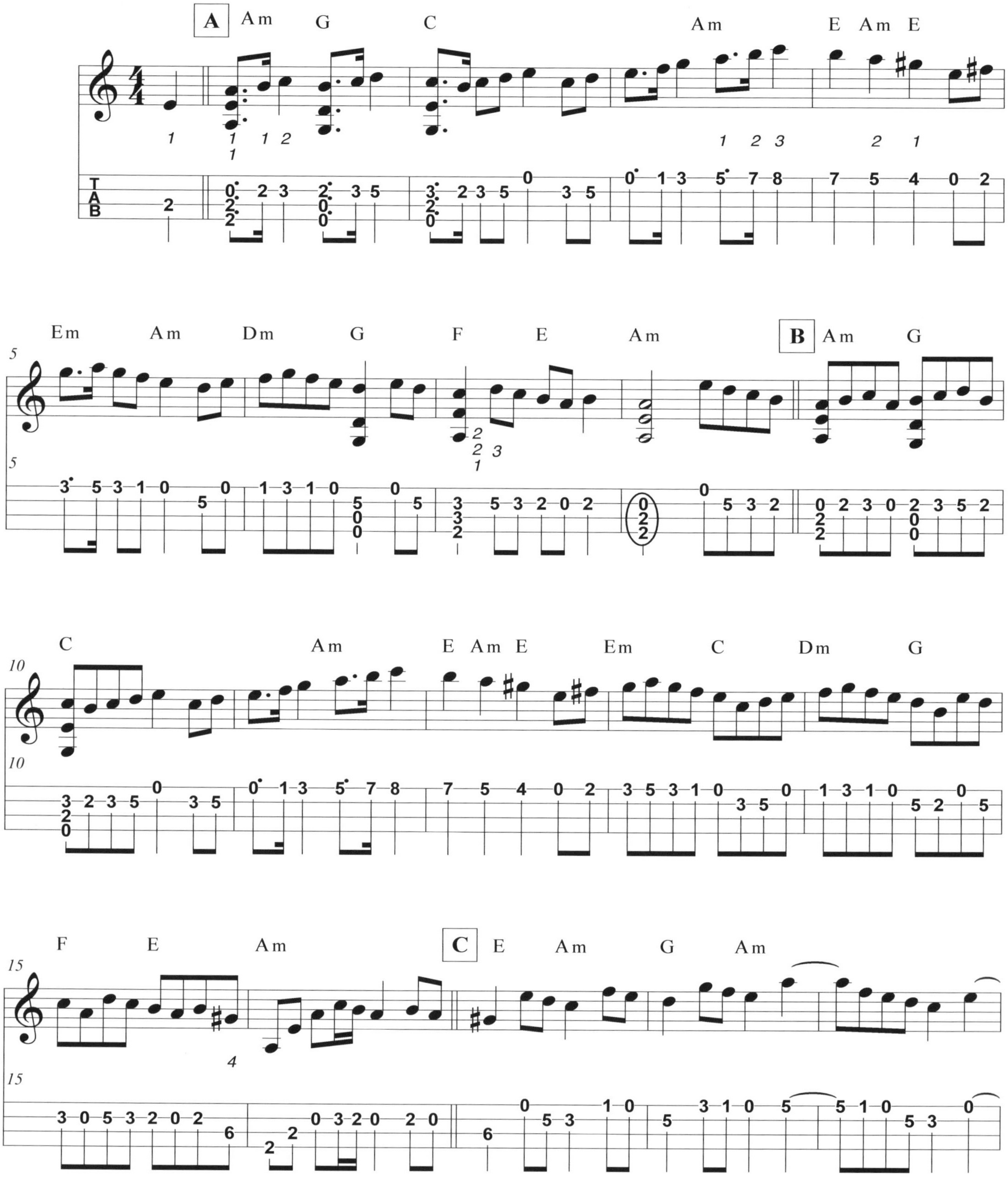

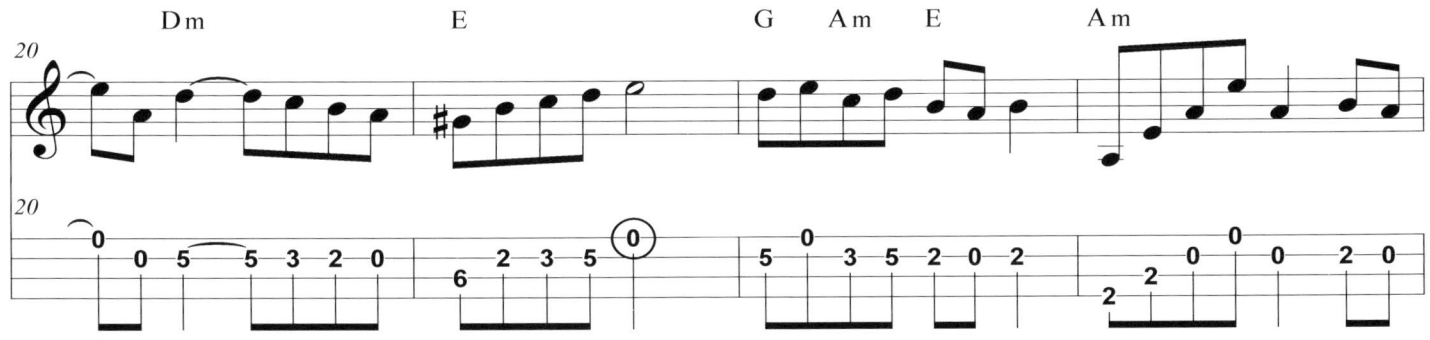
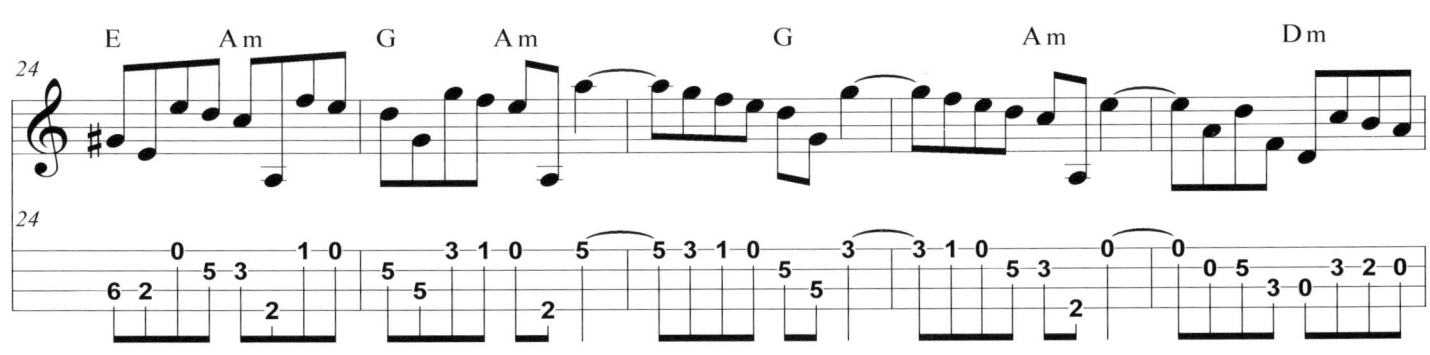
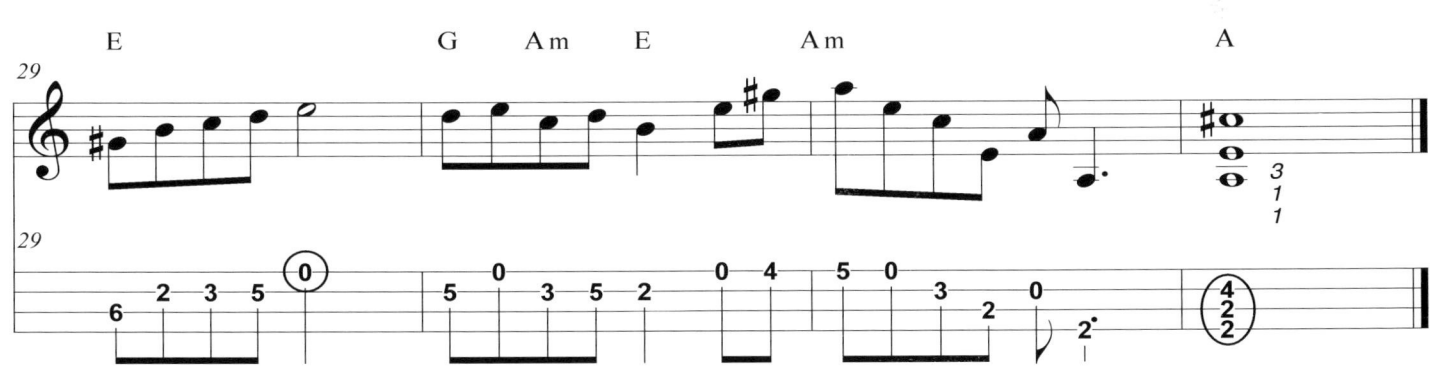

La Folias

Gaspar Sanz
Arr. by Dix Bruce

Moderato ♩ = 130

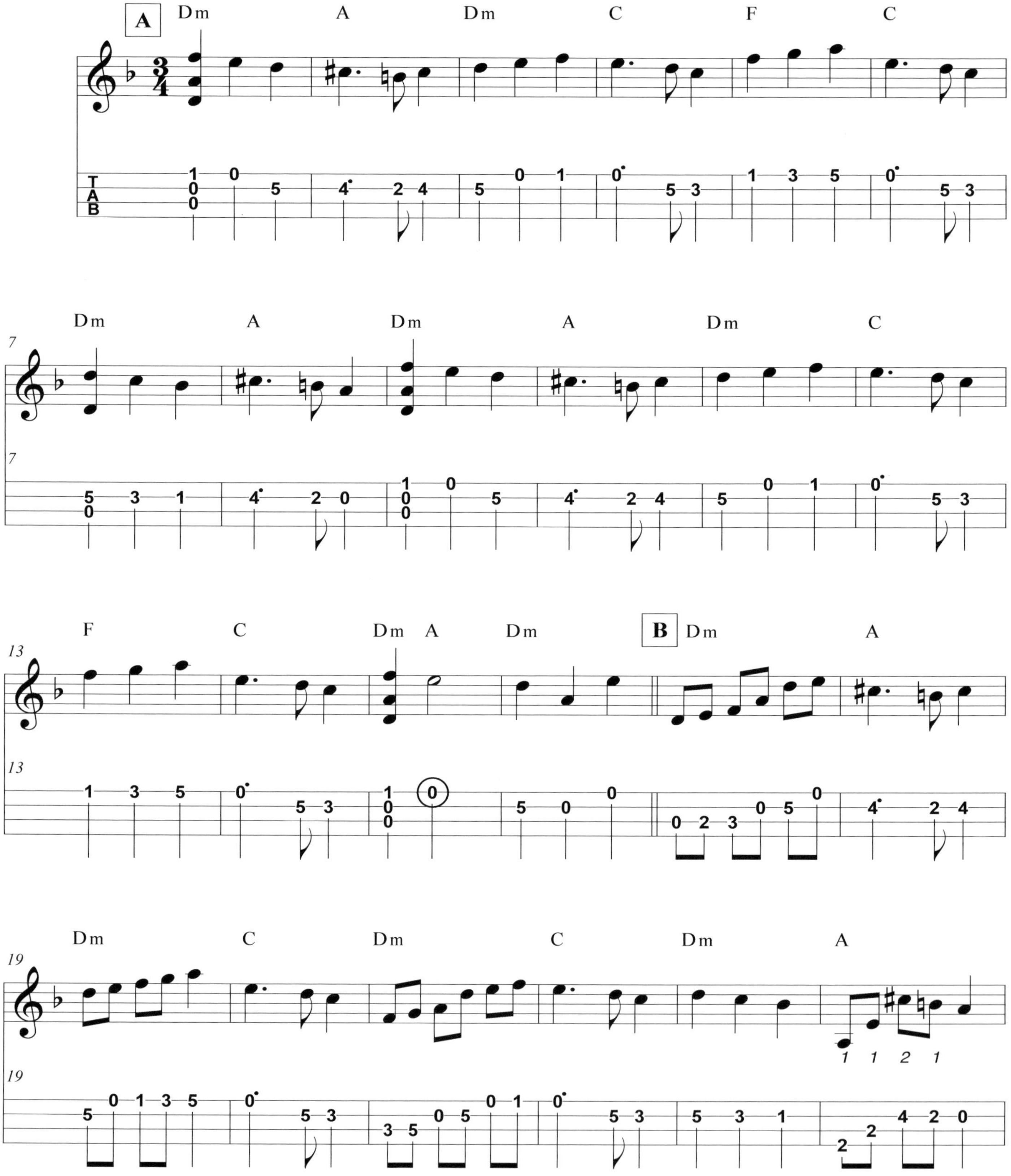

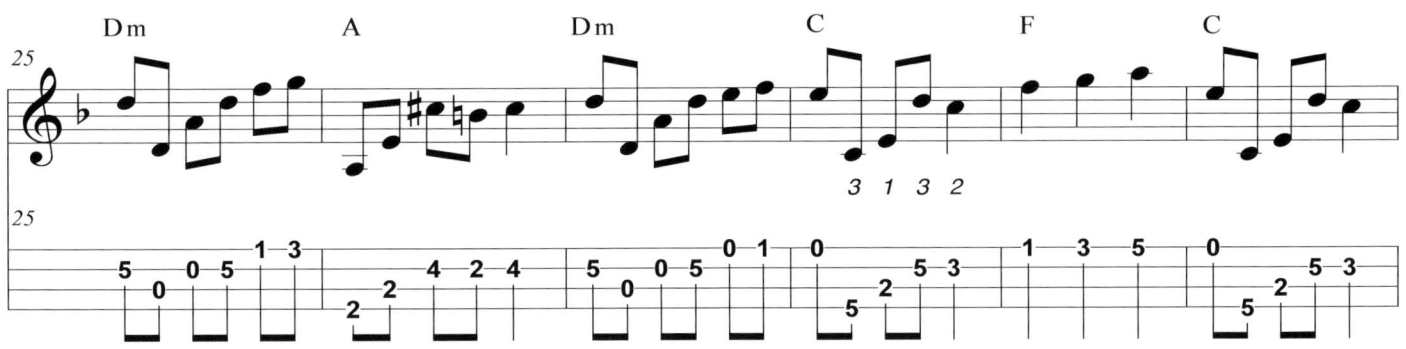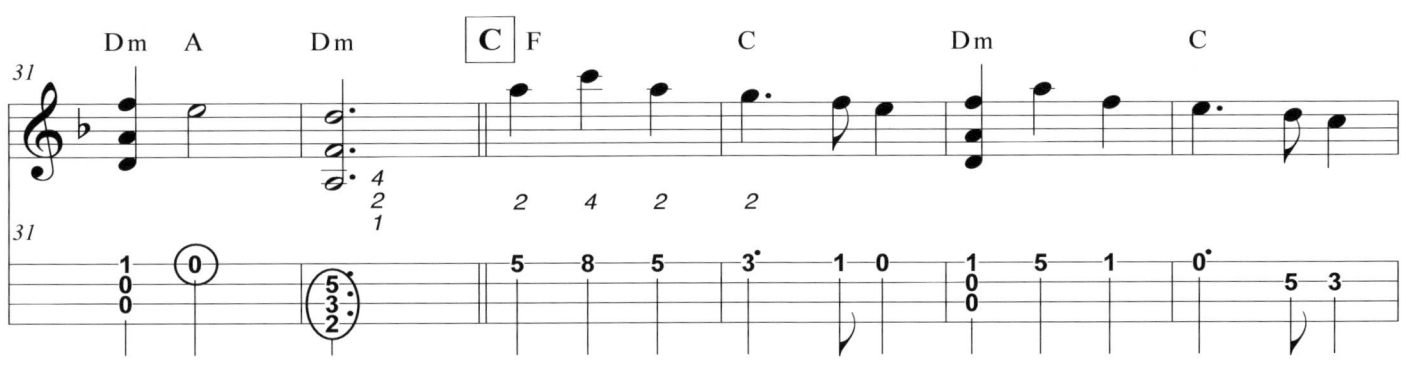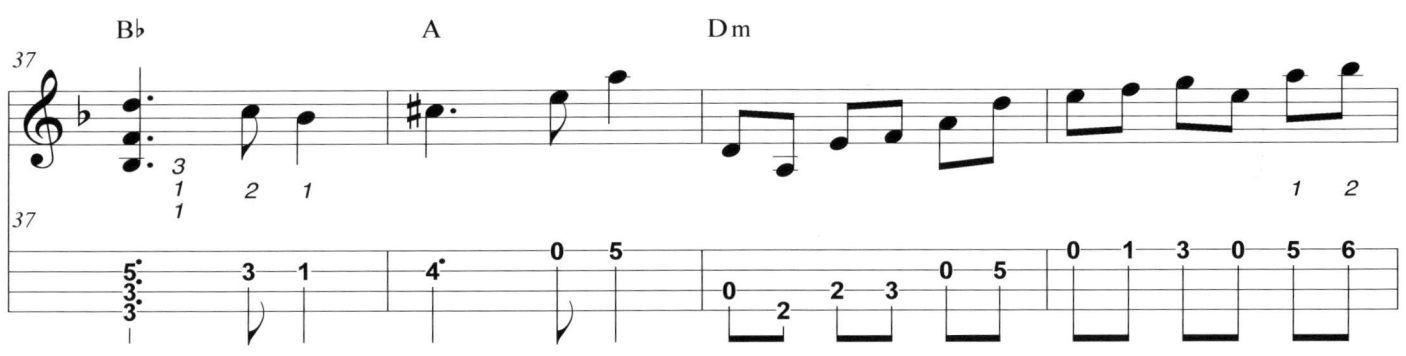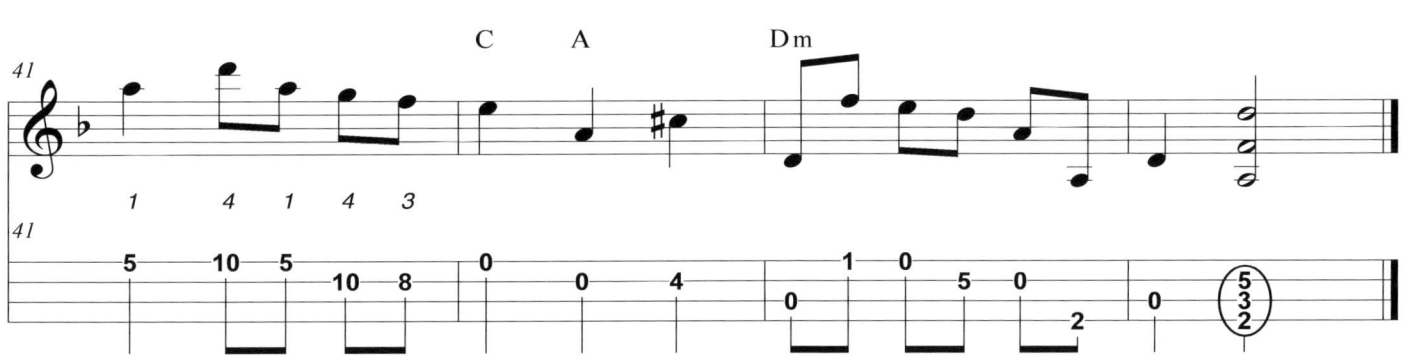

To Drive the Cold Winter Away

Moderato ♩. = 74

Unknown ca. 1625
Arr. by Dix Bruce

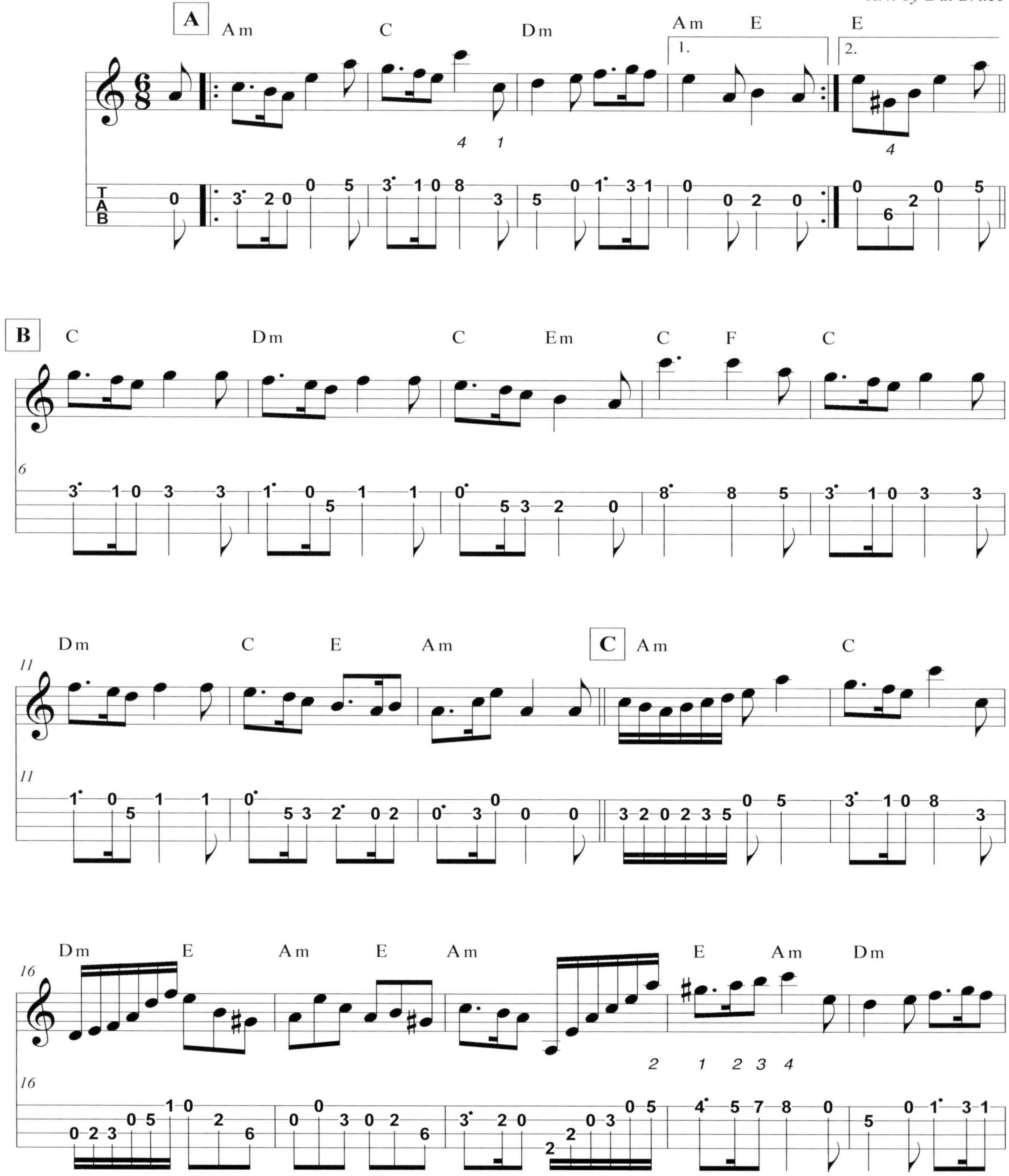

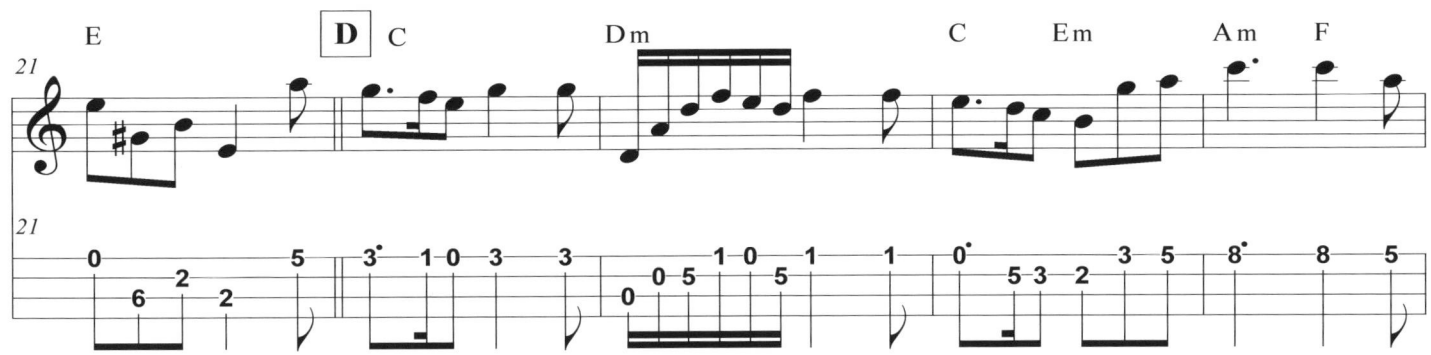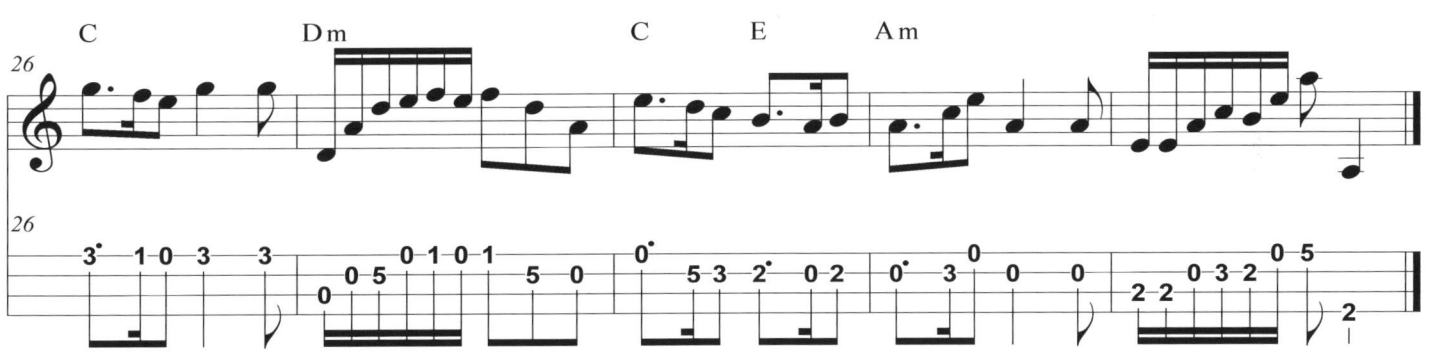

Pastourelle

13th Century French
Arr. by Dix Bruce

Allegro ♩ = 162

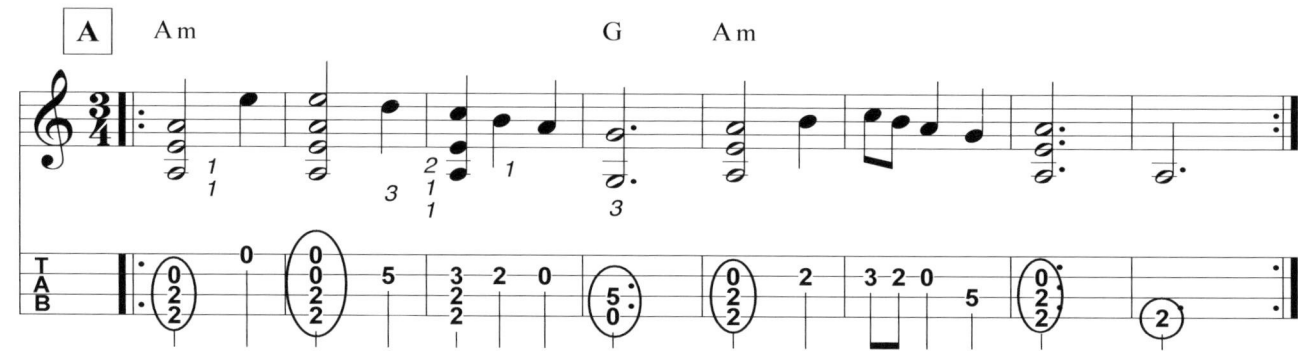
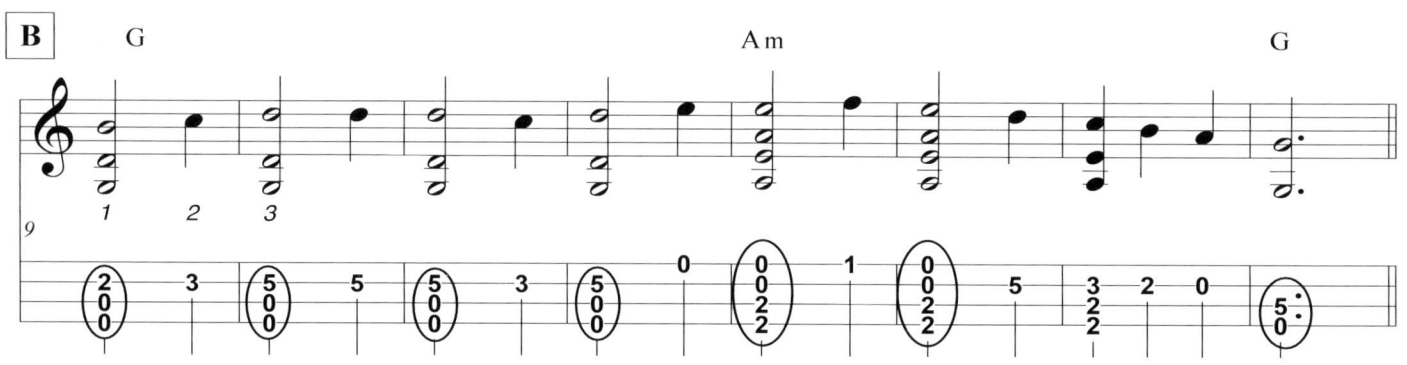
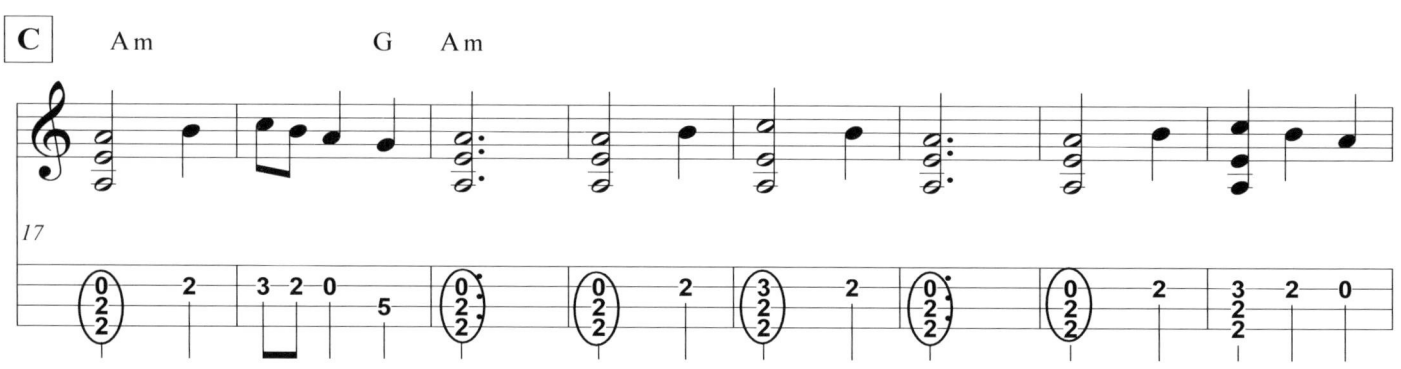
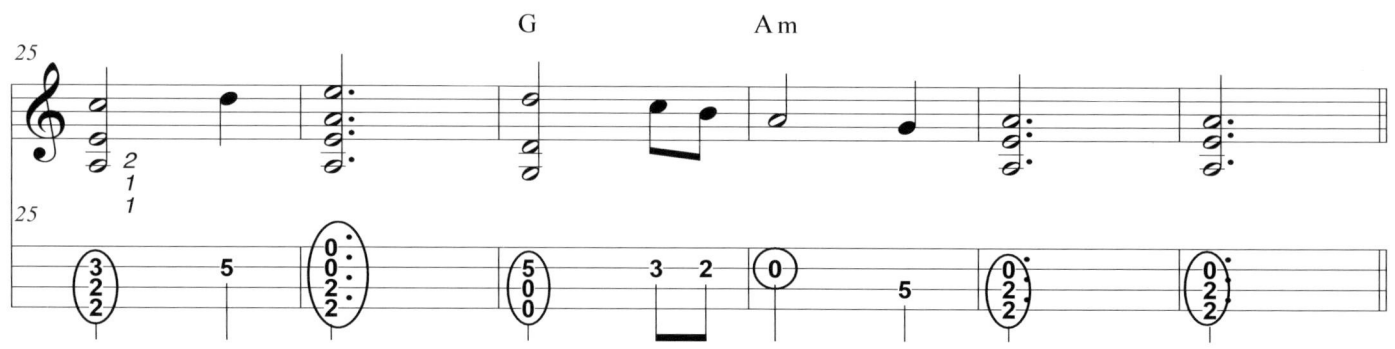

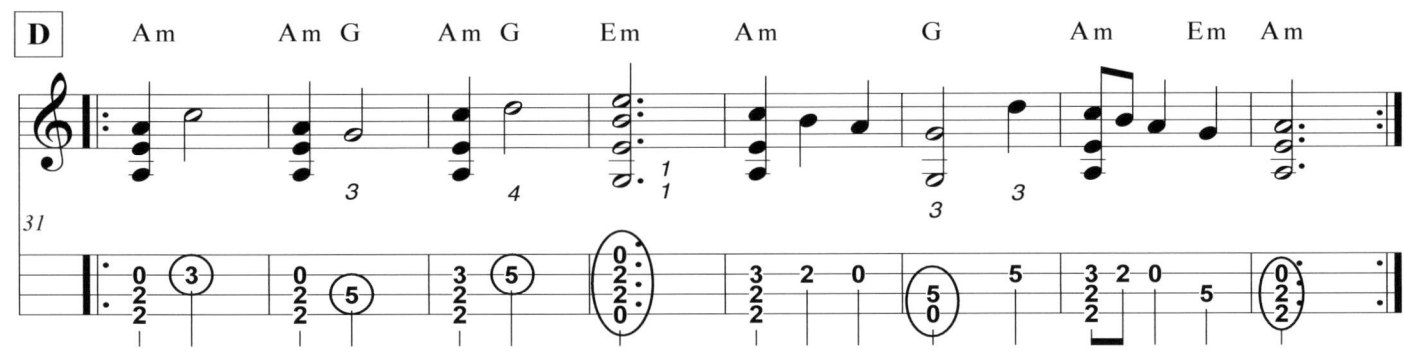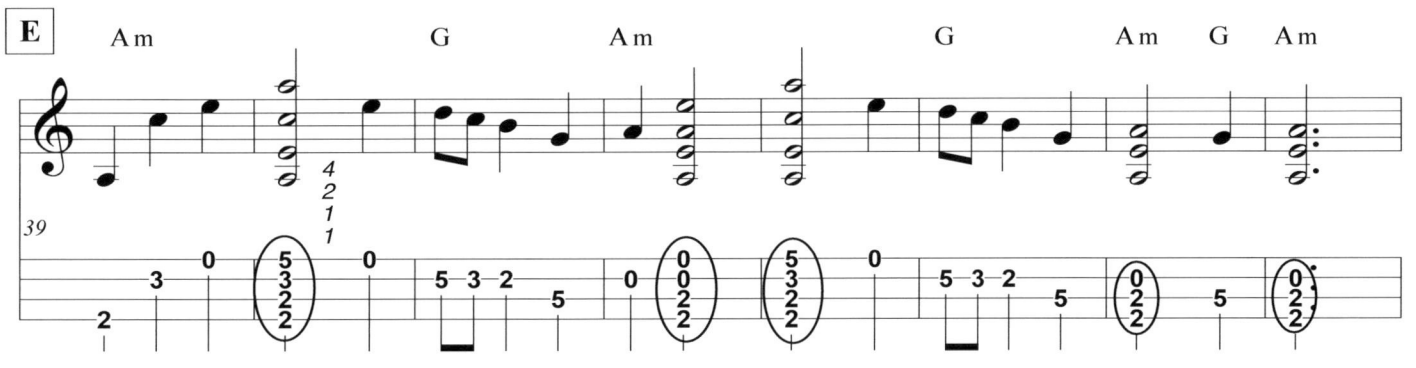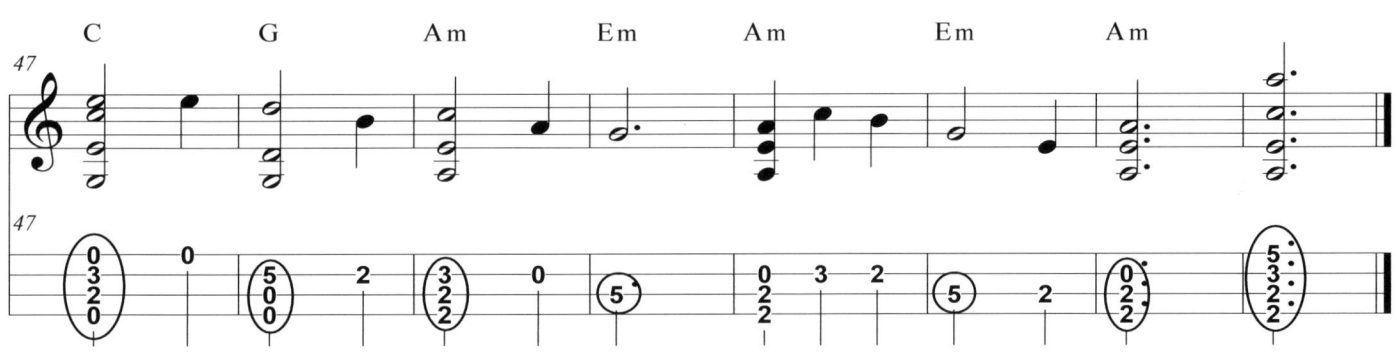

Childgrove

Rhythmically ♩=66

Playford Collection
Arr. by Dix Bruce

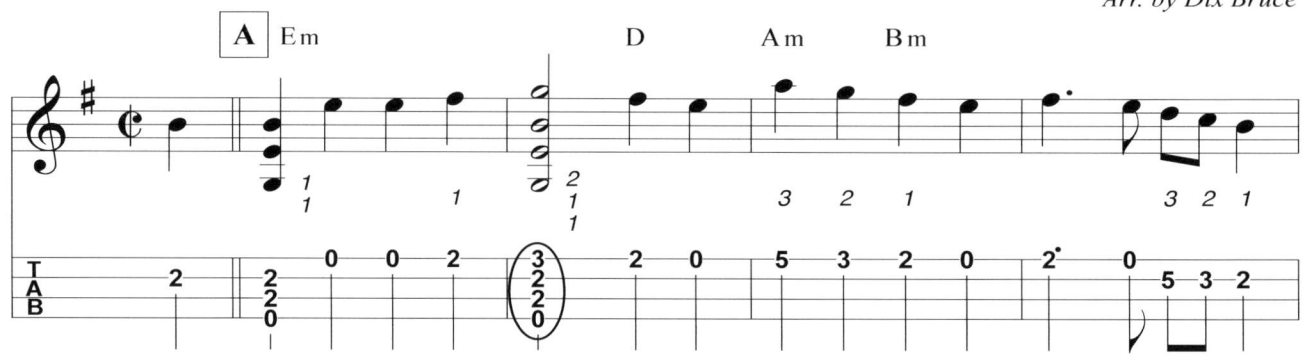
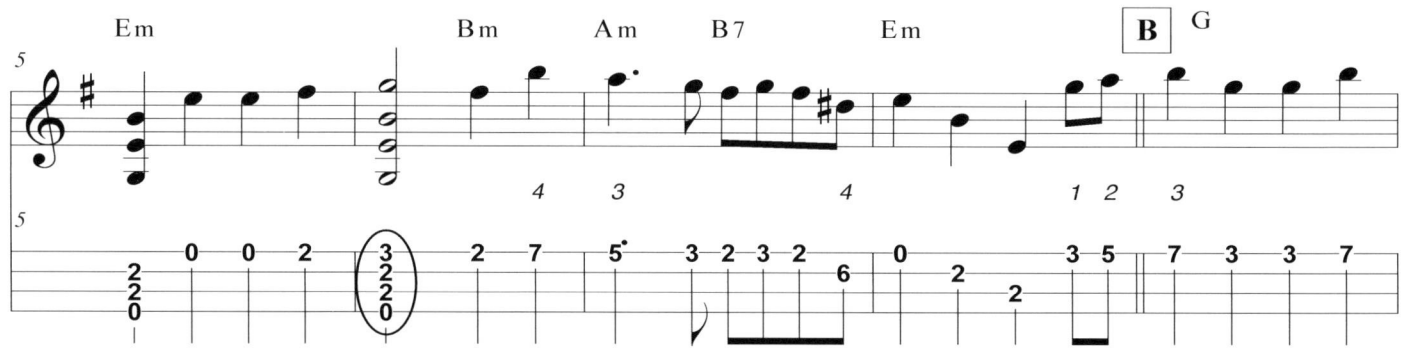
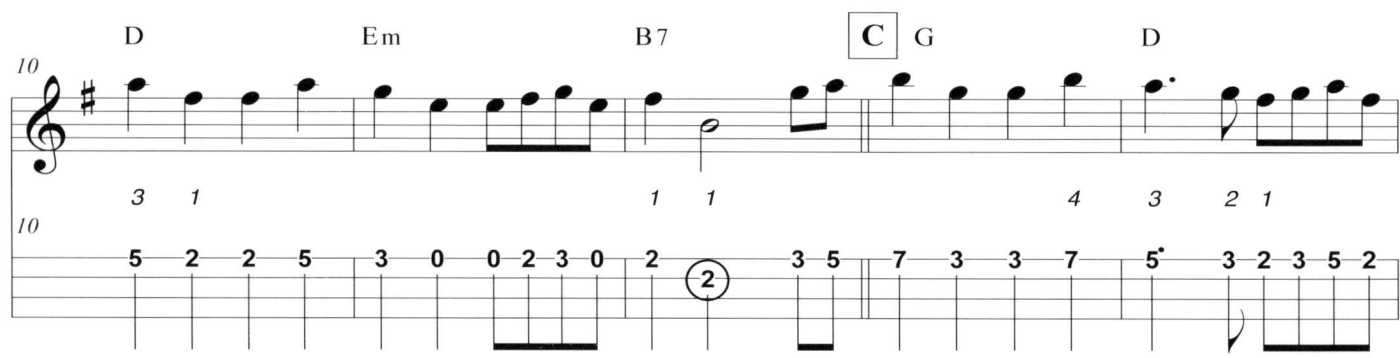
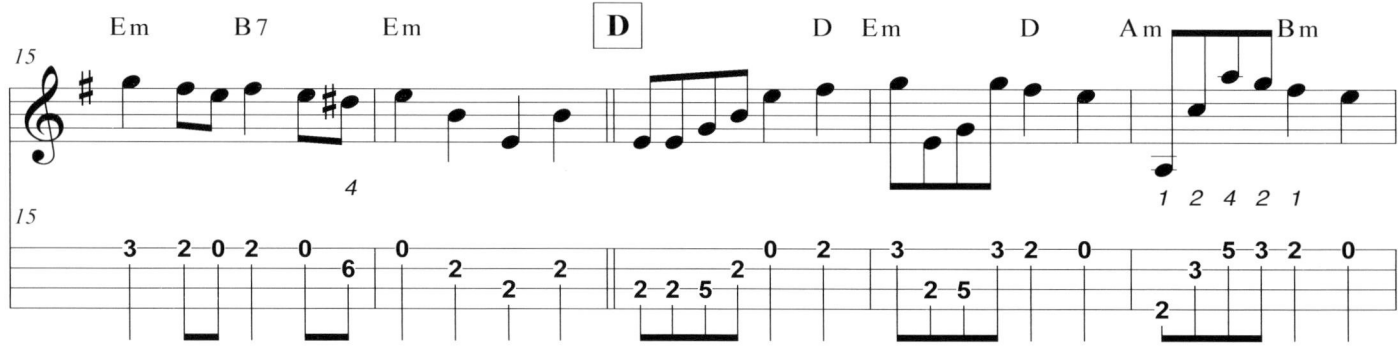

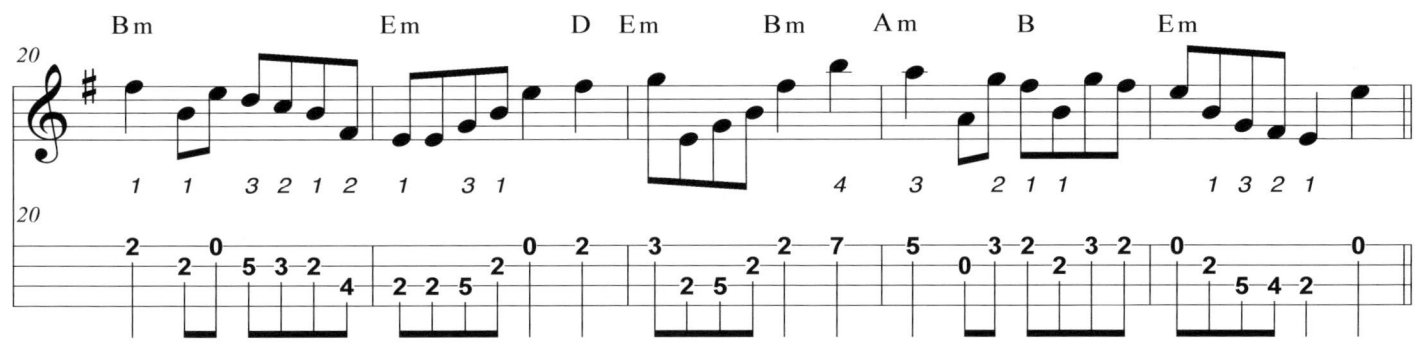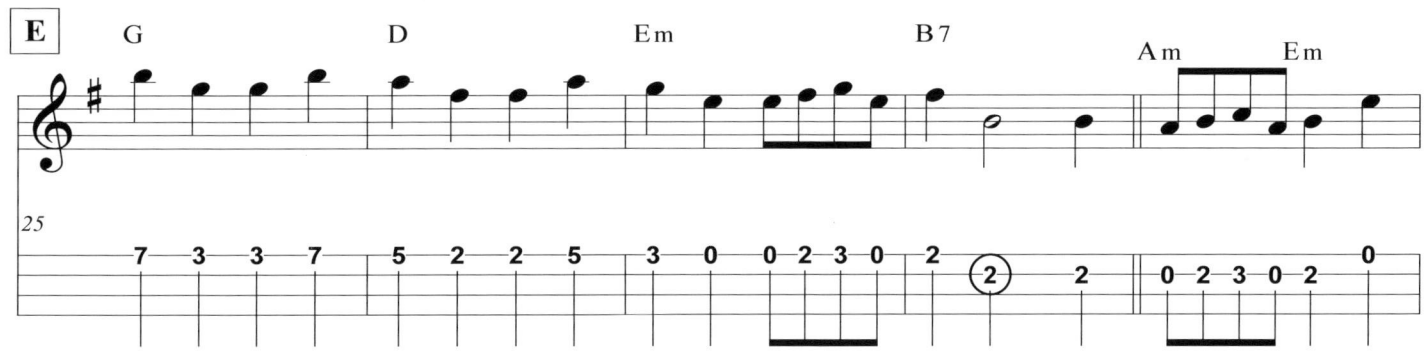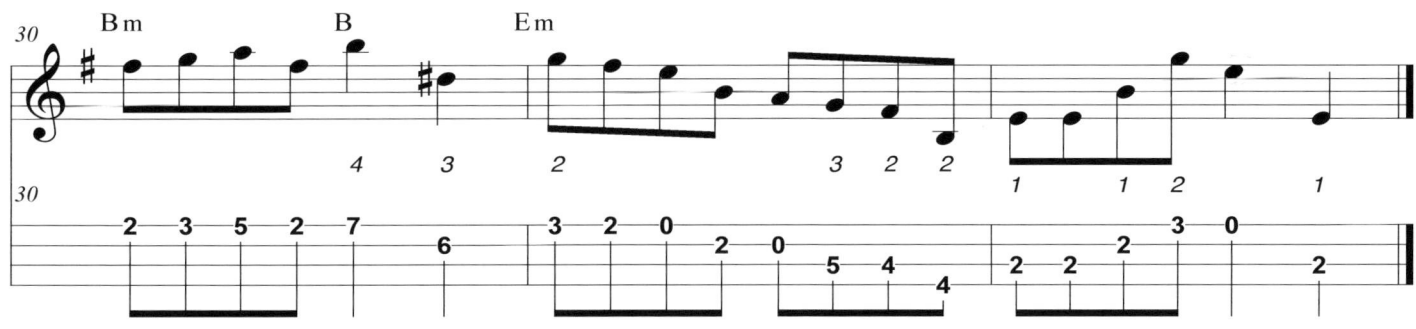

Allegro Lute

Anonymous
Arr. by Dix Bruce

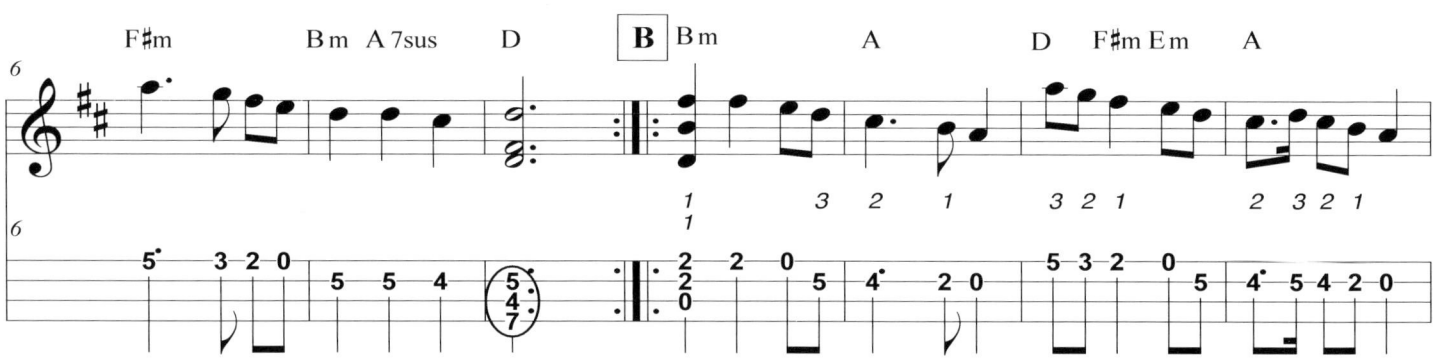
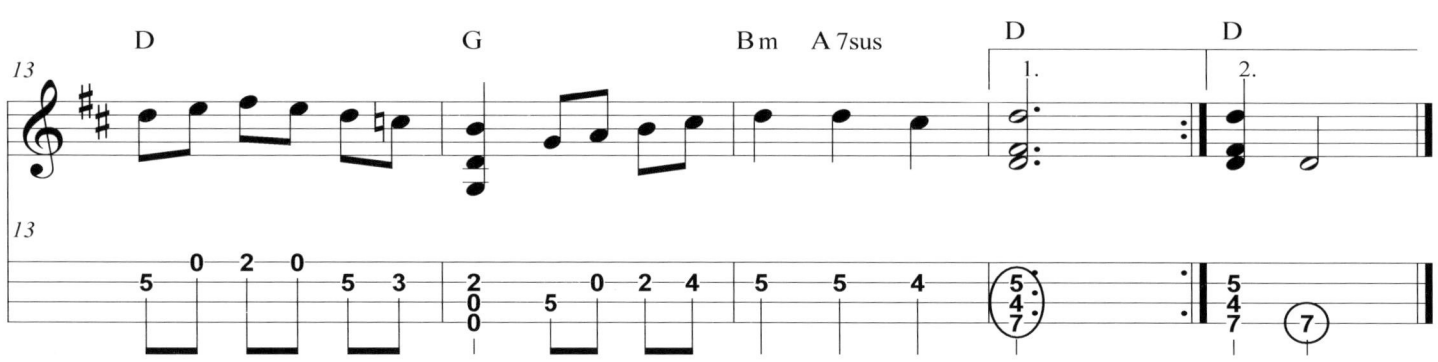

St. Martins

Moderato ♩ = 126

John Playford
Arr. by Dix Bruce

Moderato Lute

Unknown
Arr. by Dix Bruce

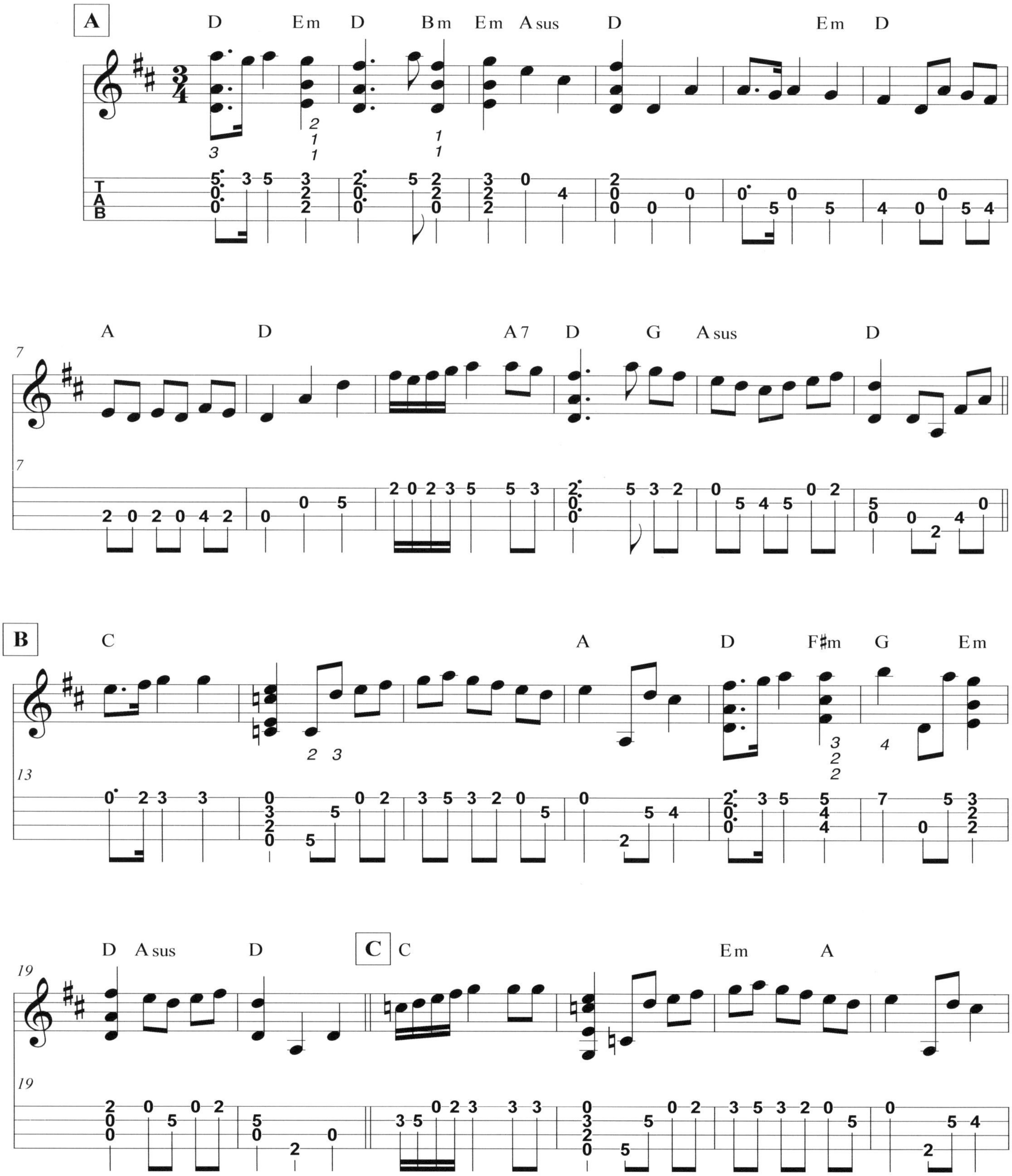

Moderato ♩ = 88

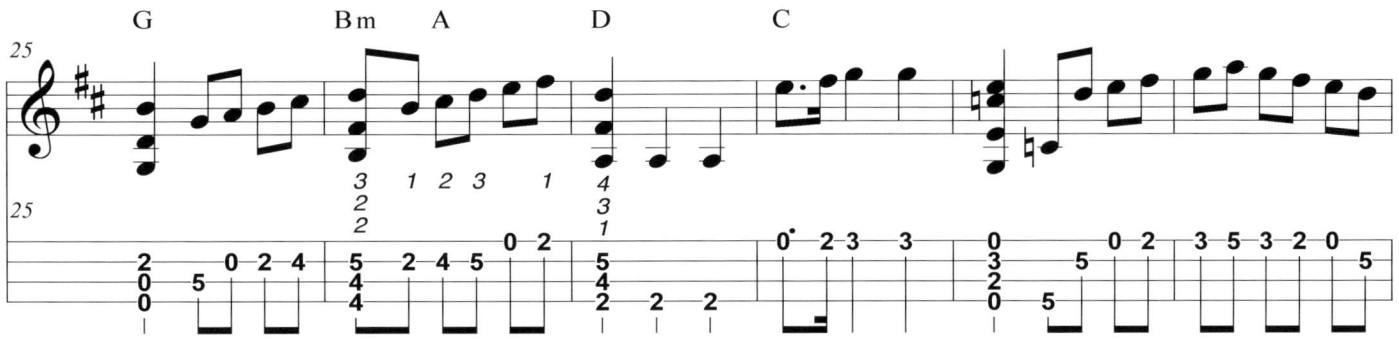
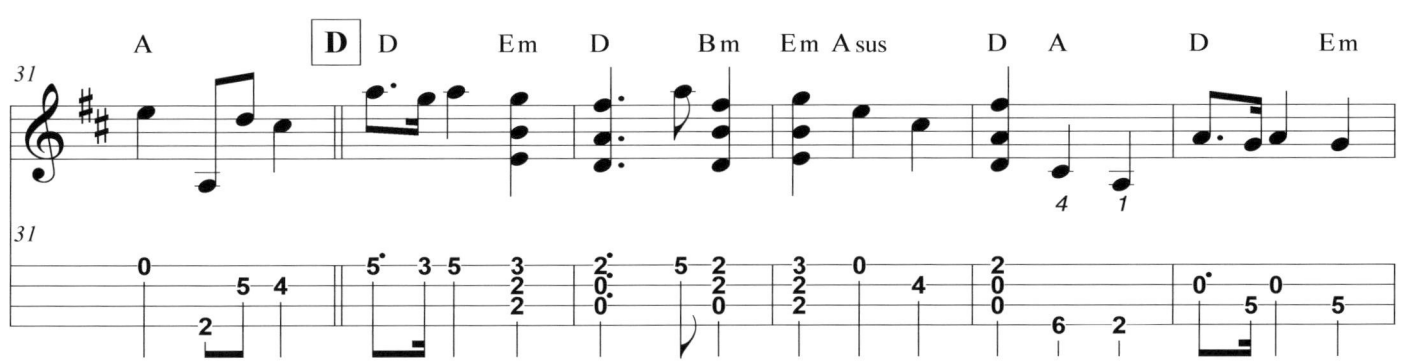
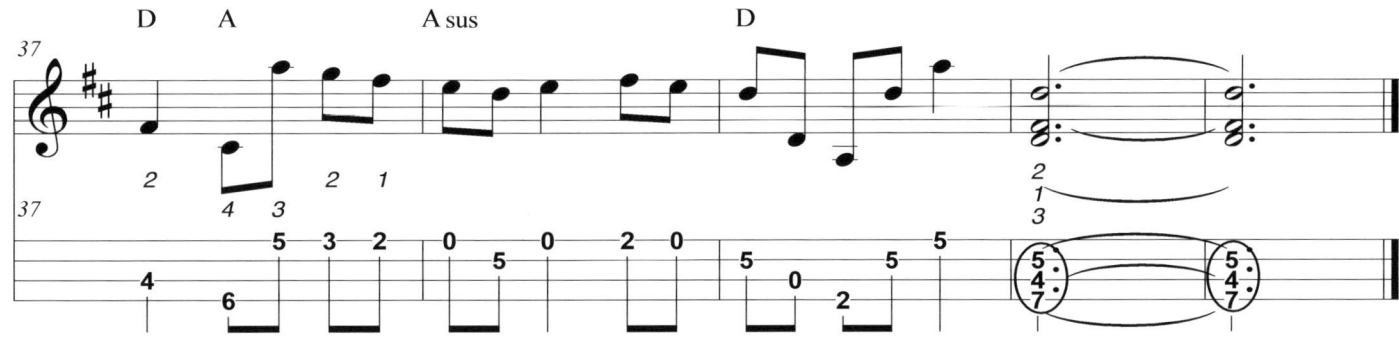

45

Come with Me, My Giselle

Andante ♩ = 74

Adam de la Halle
Arr. by Dix Bruce

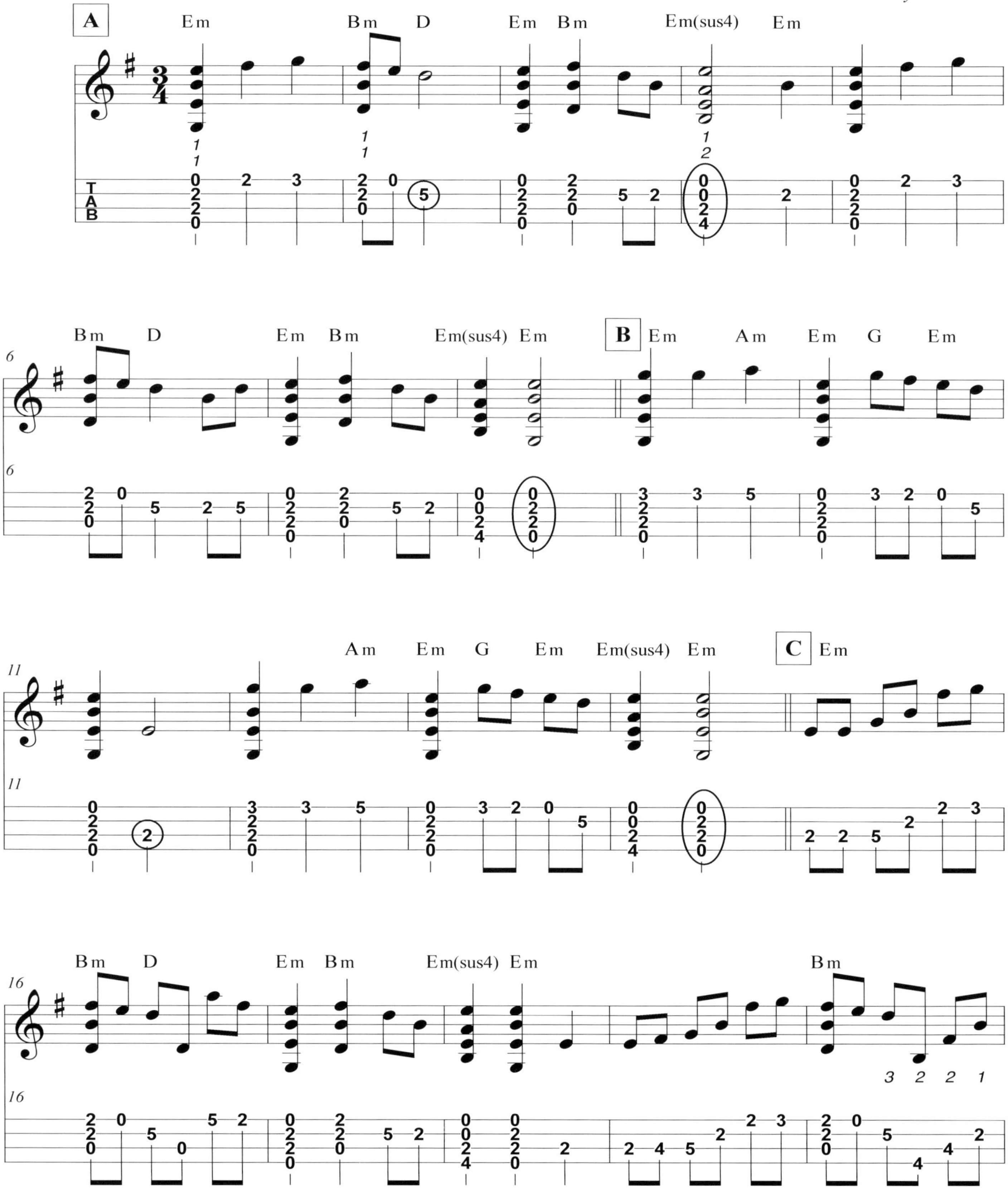

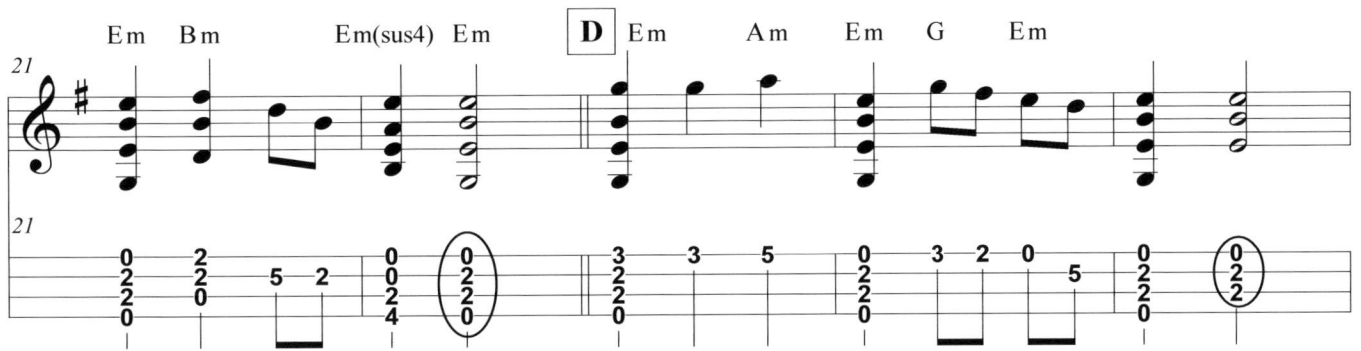
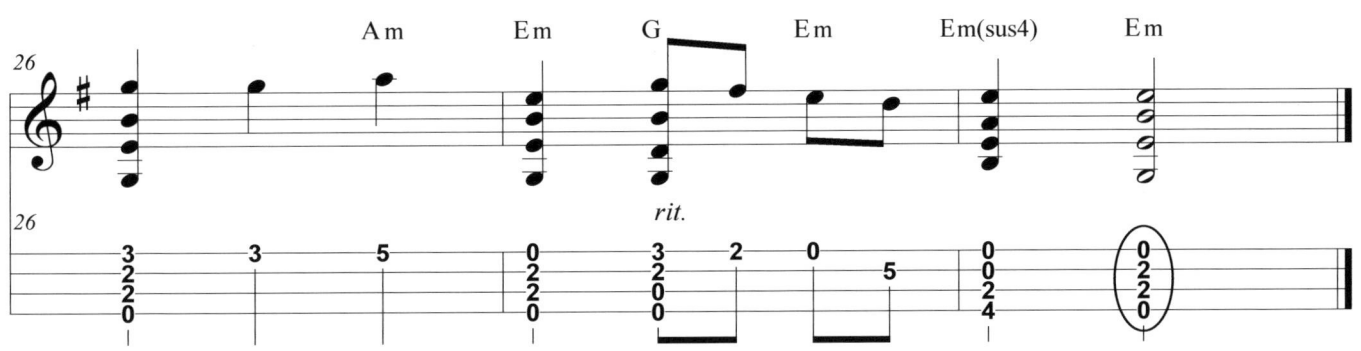

47

O Esca Viatorum

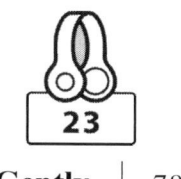

Gently ♩ = 78

Louis Bourgeois 1549
Arr. by Dix Bruce

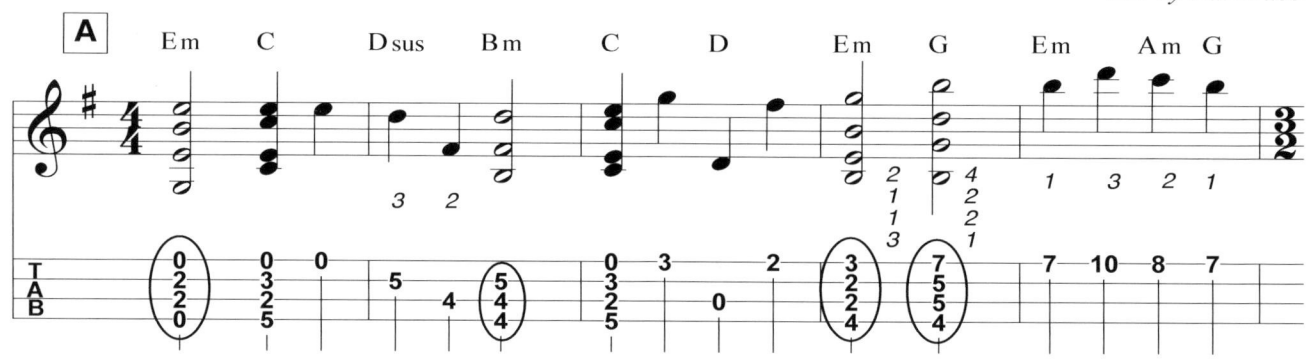
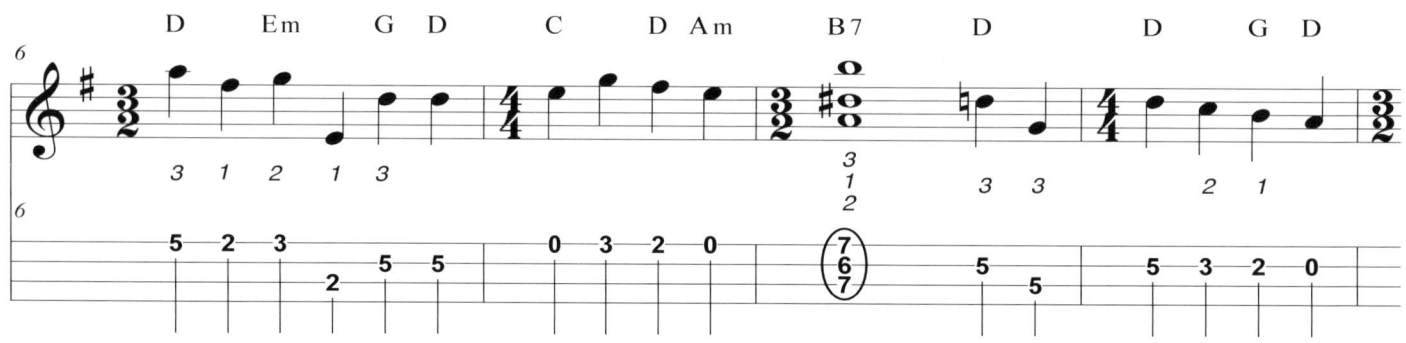
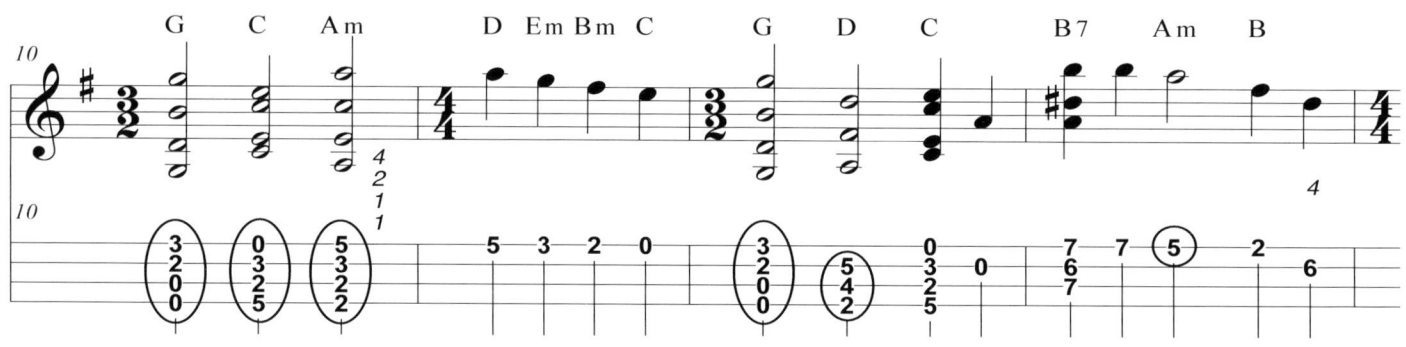
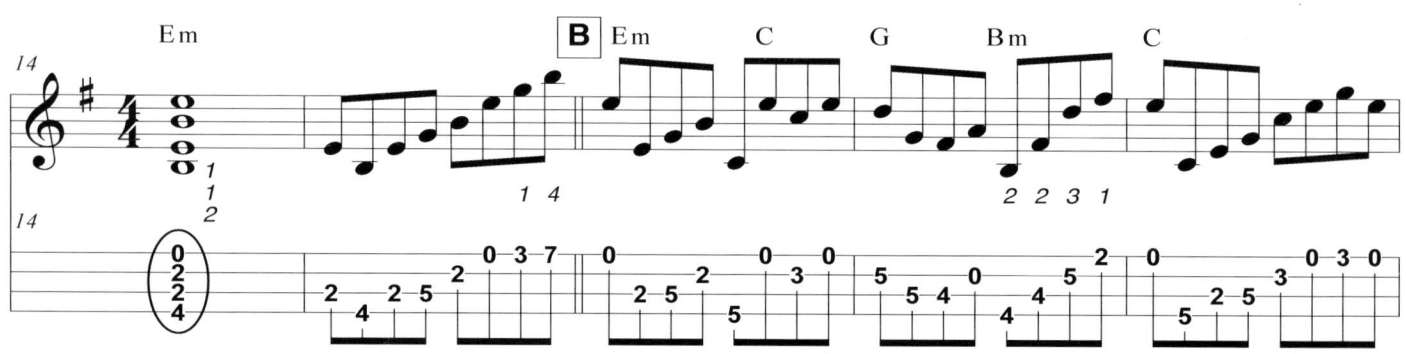

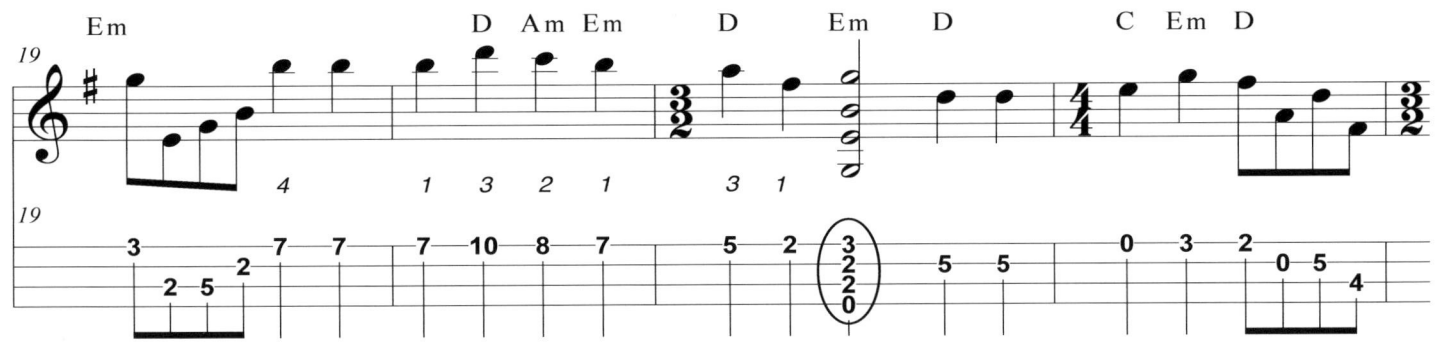
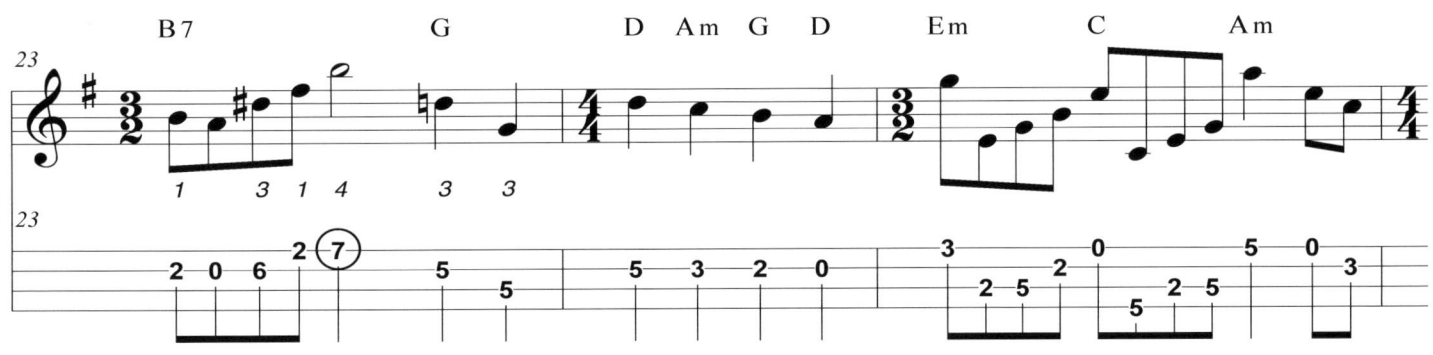
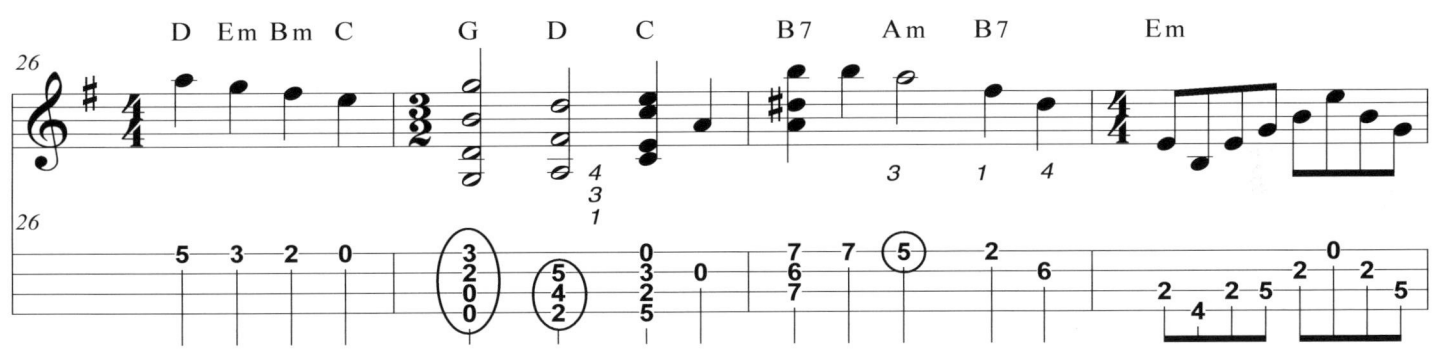
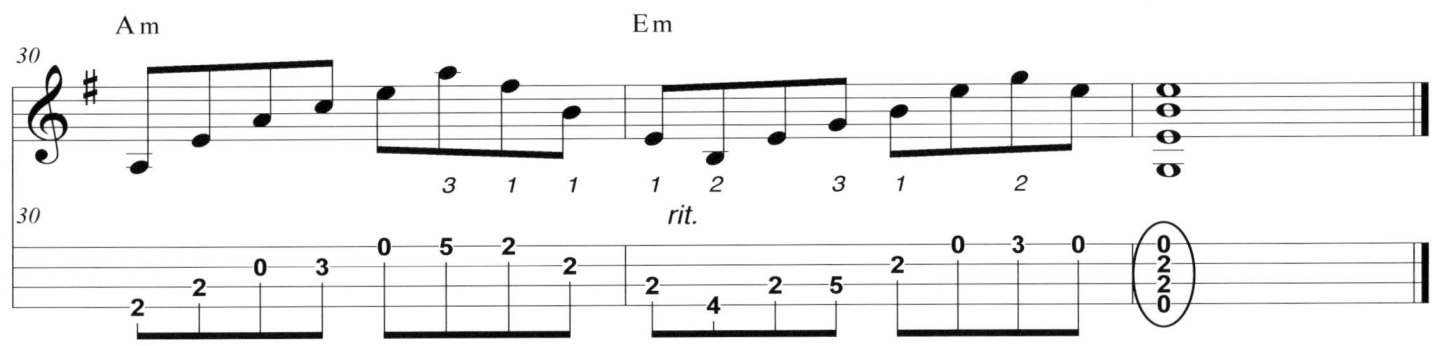

Volte

Allegro ♩ = 128

Michael Praetorius
Arr. by Dix Bruce

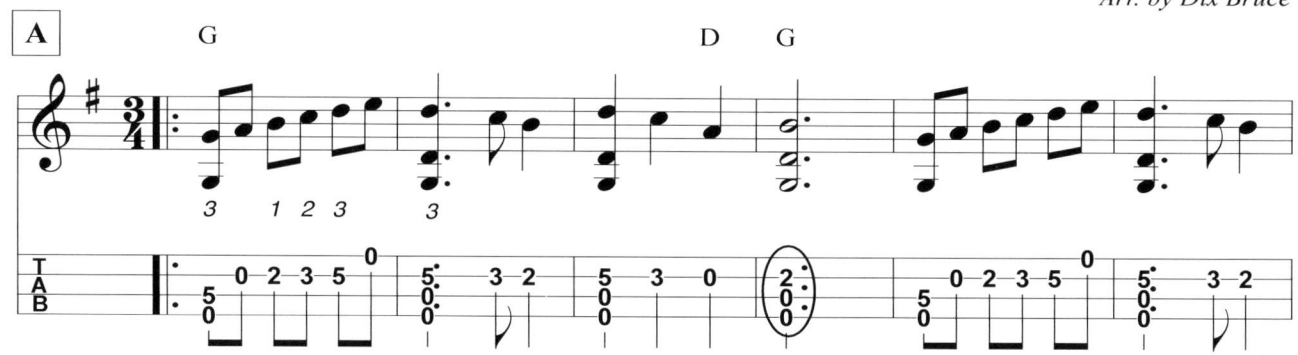
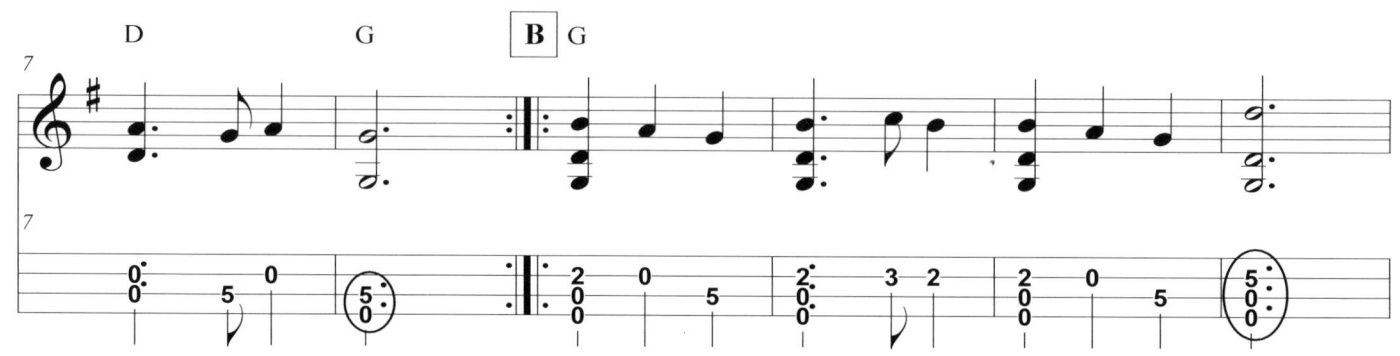
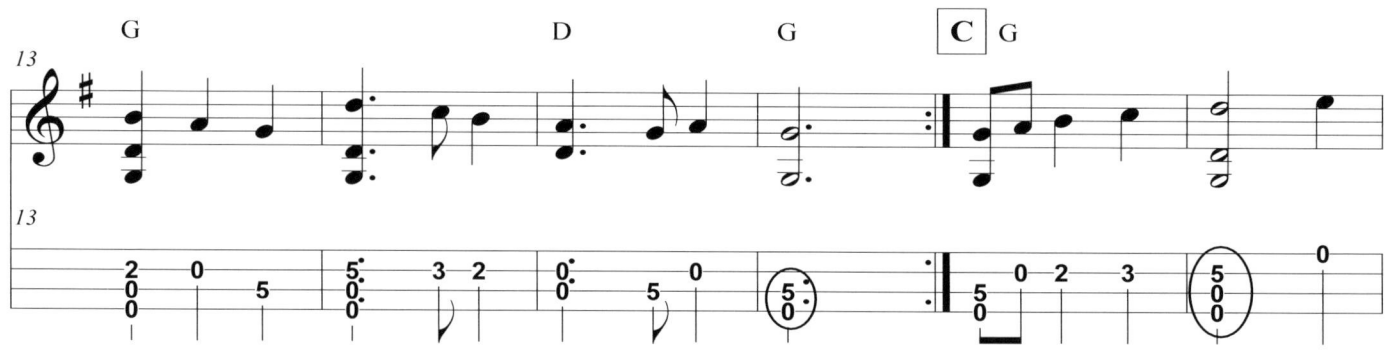
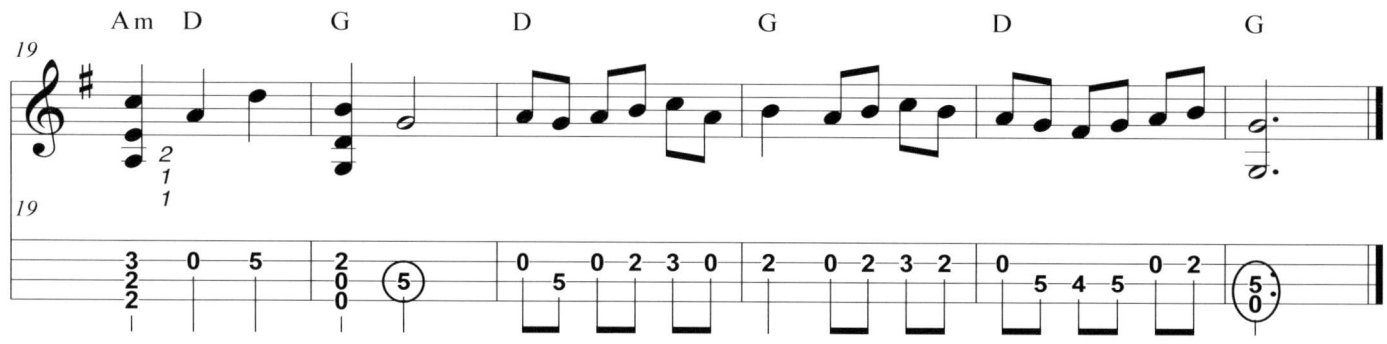

25

Tutte Venite Armati

Moderato ♩ = 116

Giovanni Gastoldi
Arr. by Dix Bruce

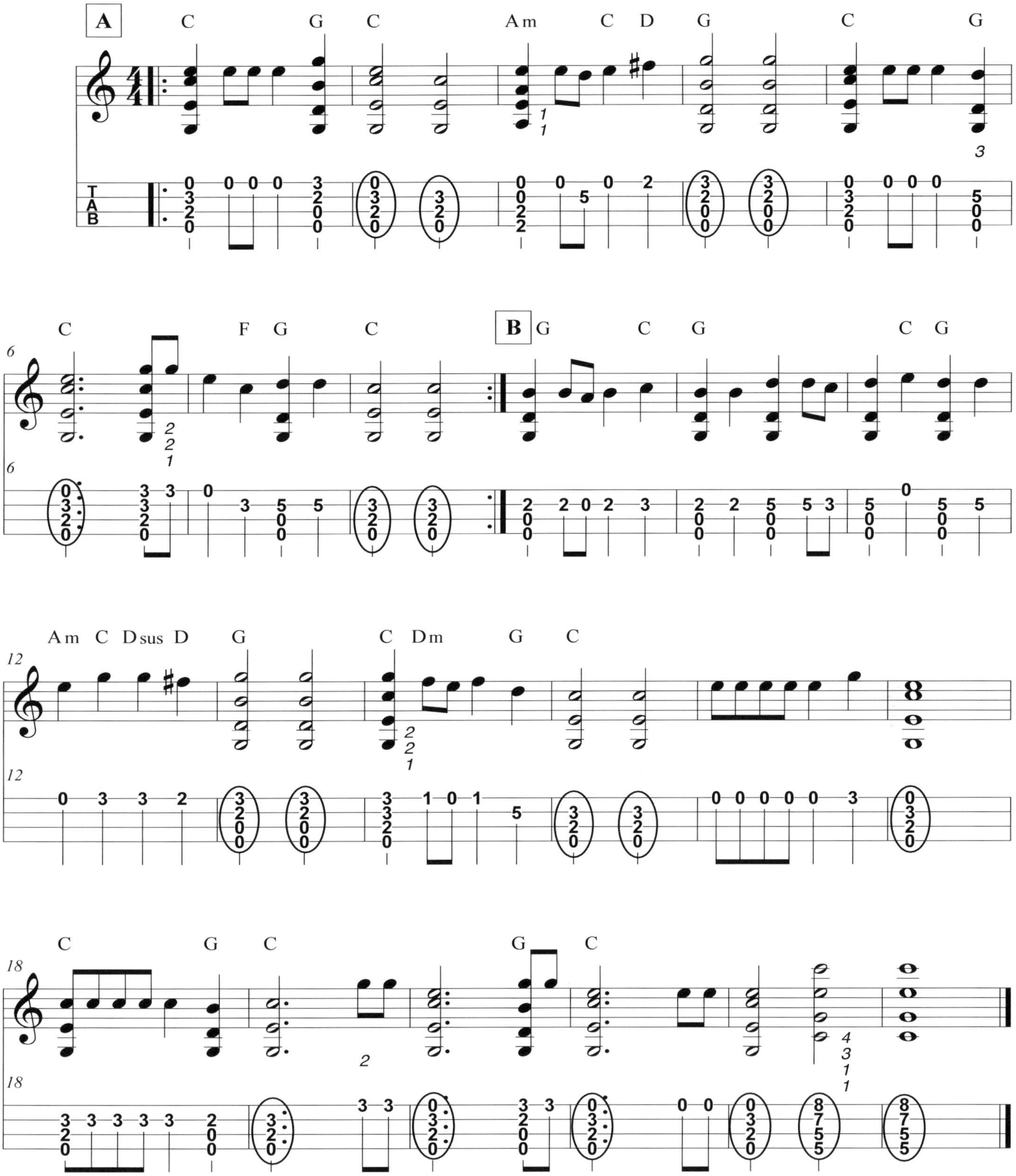

Grimstock

John Playford
Arr. by Dix Bruce

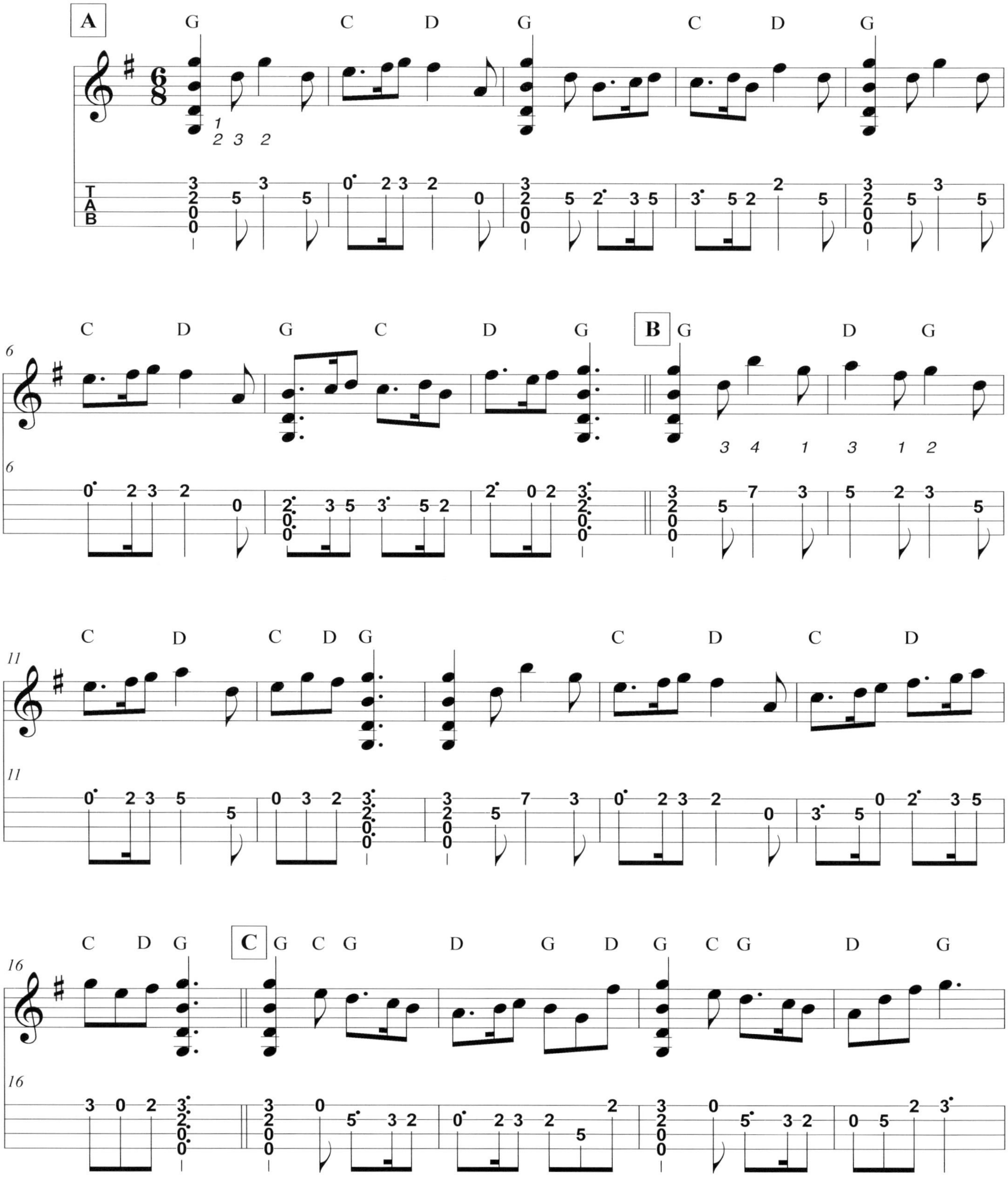

Allegro ♩. = 64

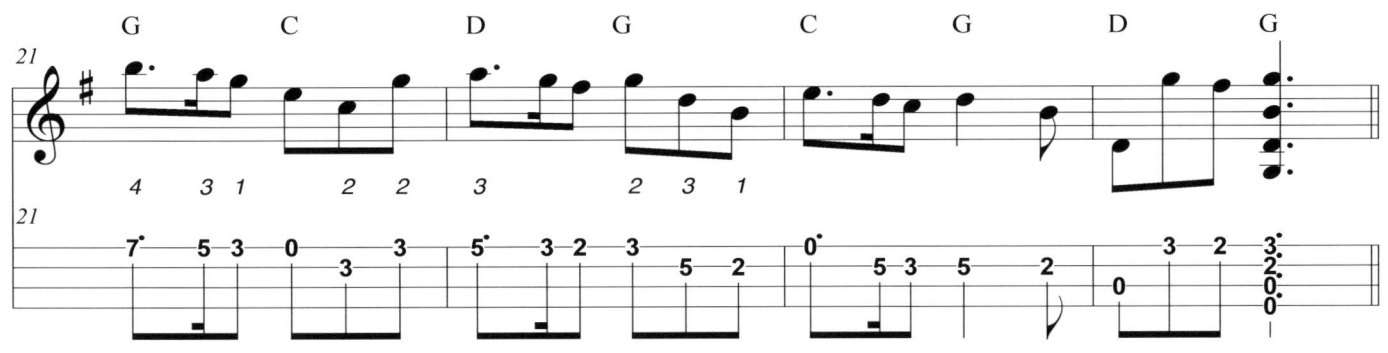
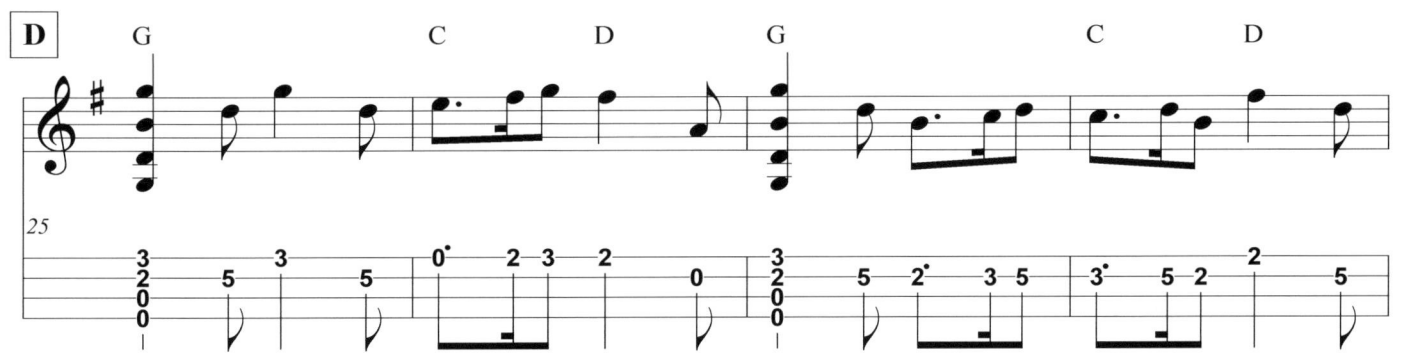
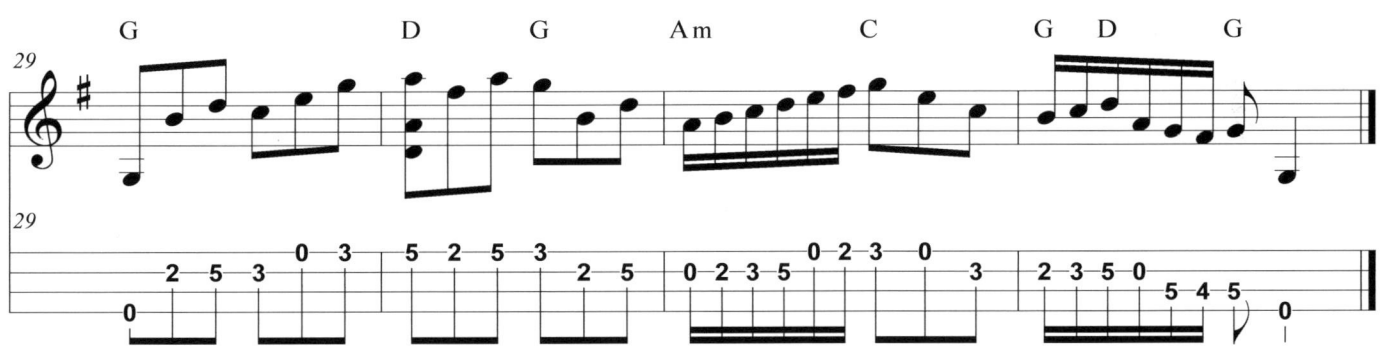

Dont vient cela

Susato 1551
danserye
Arr. by Dix Bruce

Moderato ♩ = 128

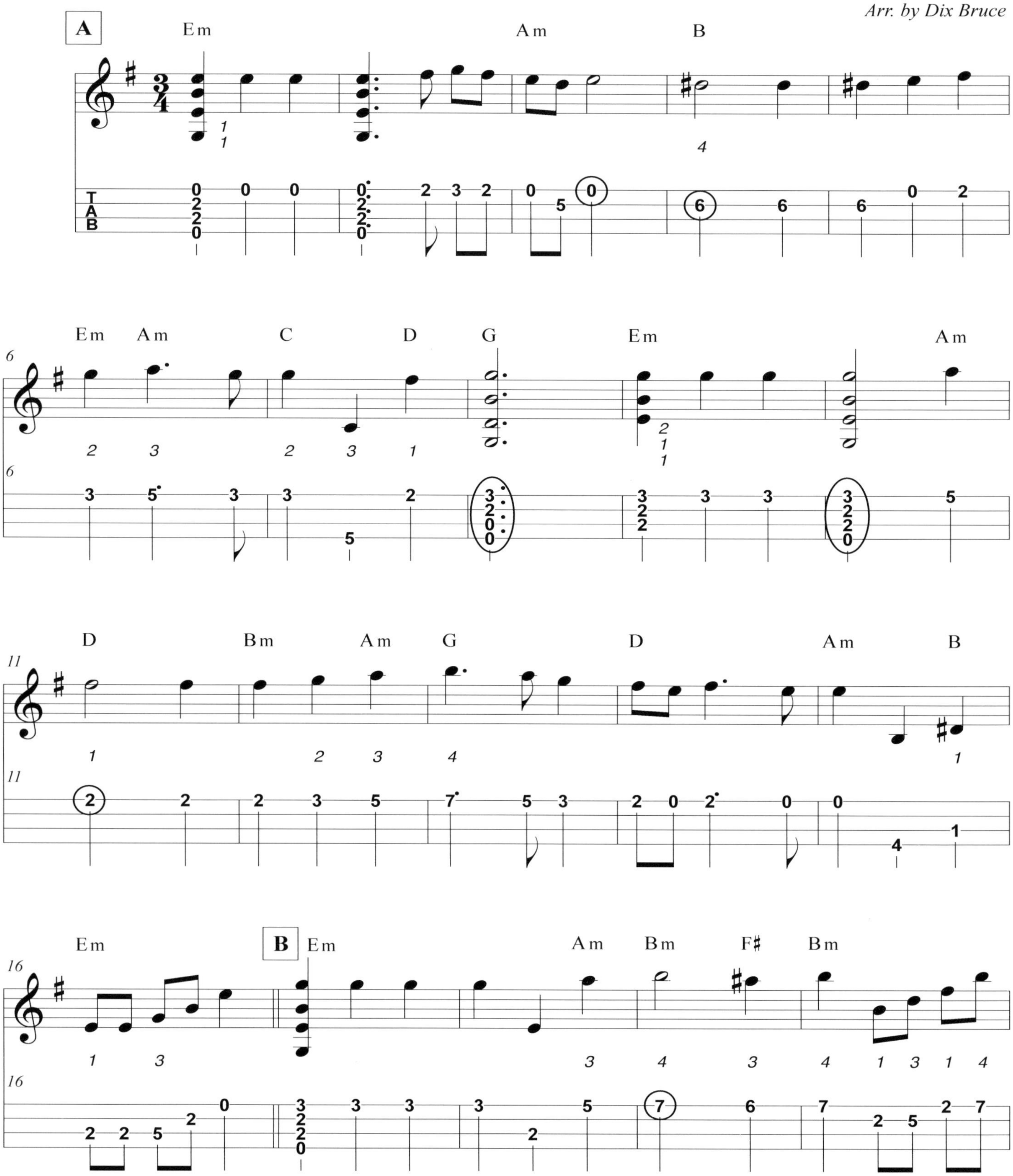

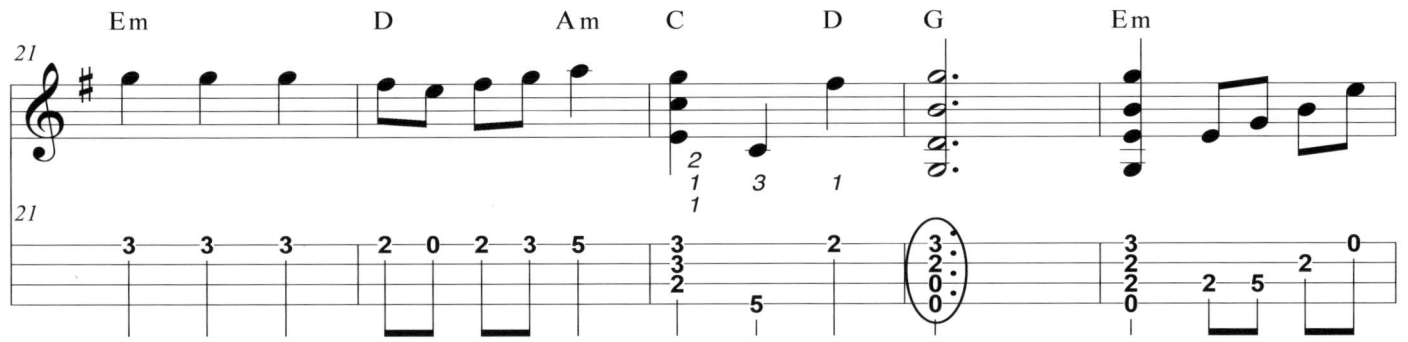
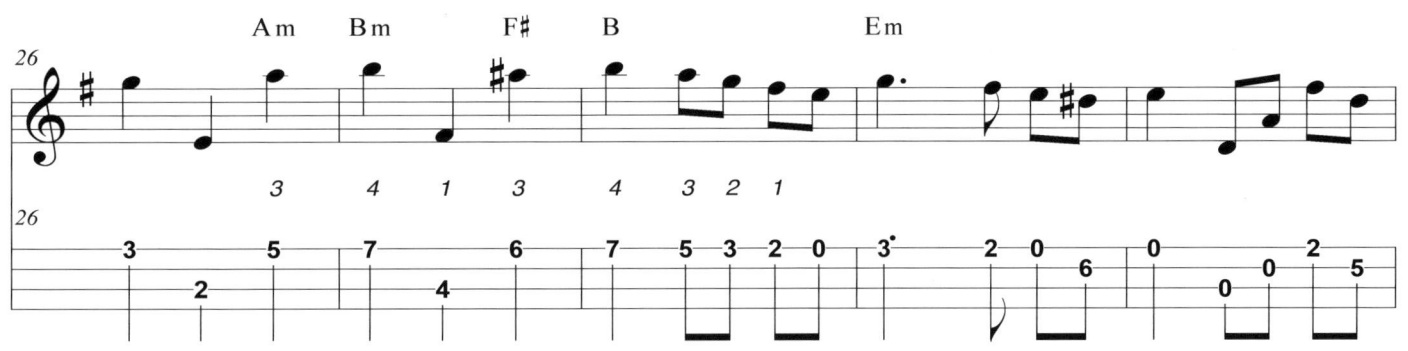
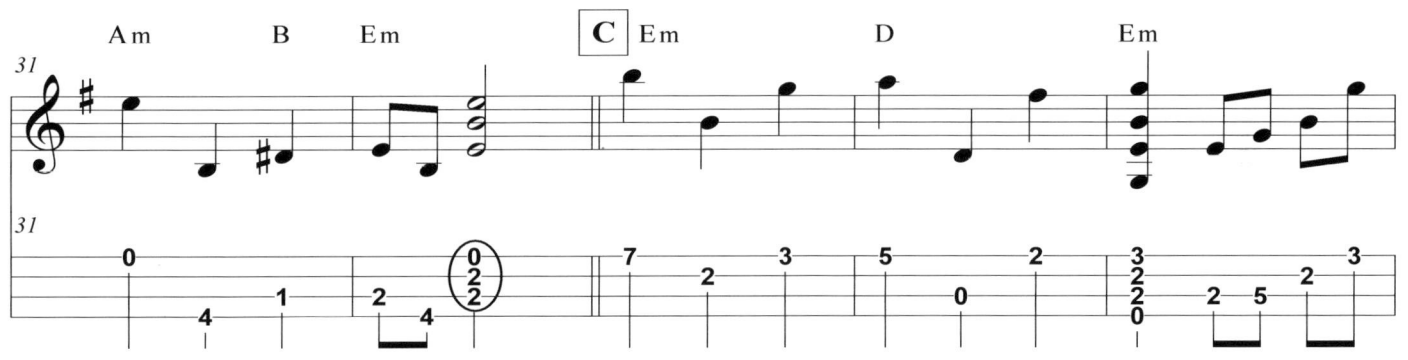
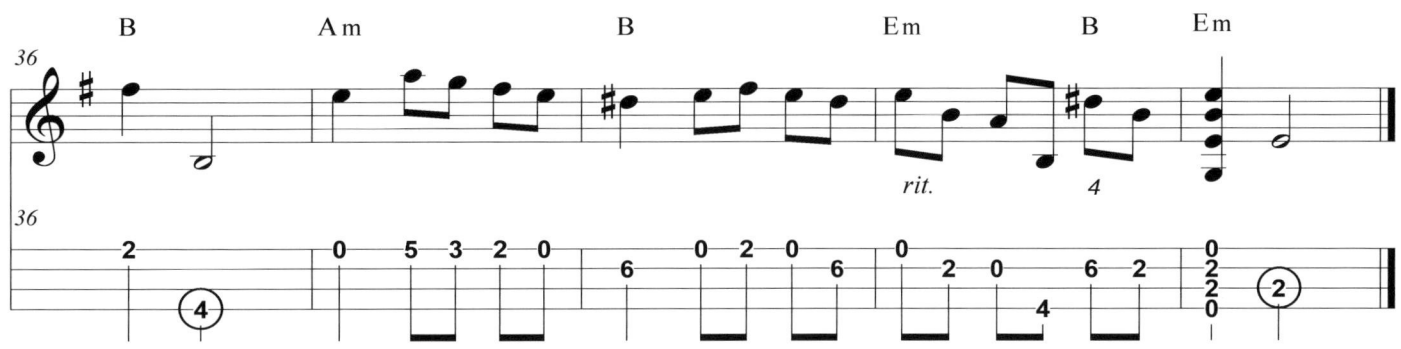

Fortune My Foe

John Dowland
Arr. by Dix Bruce

Moderato ♩ = 110

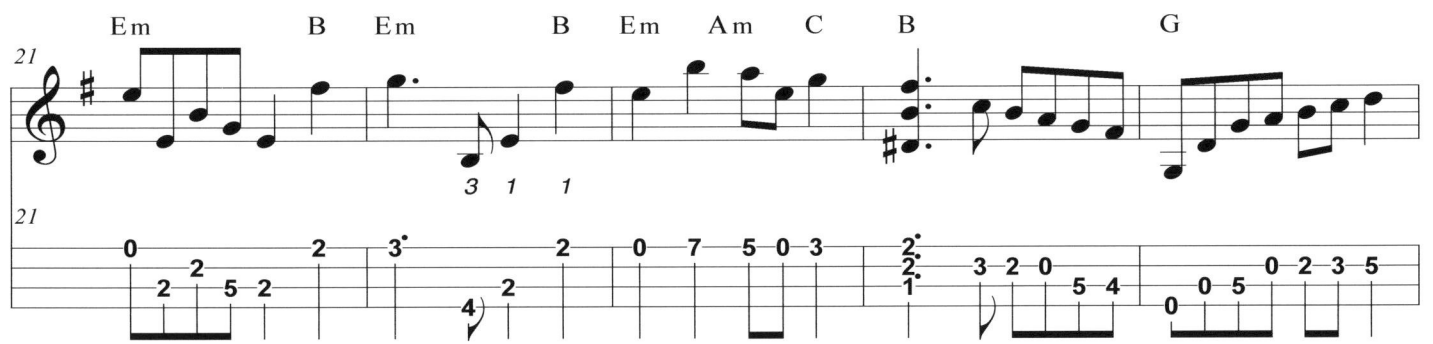
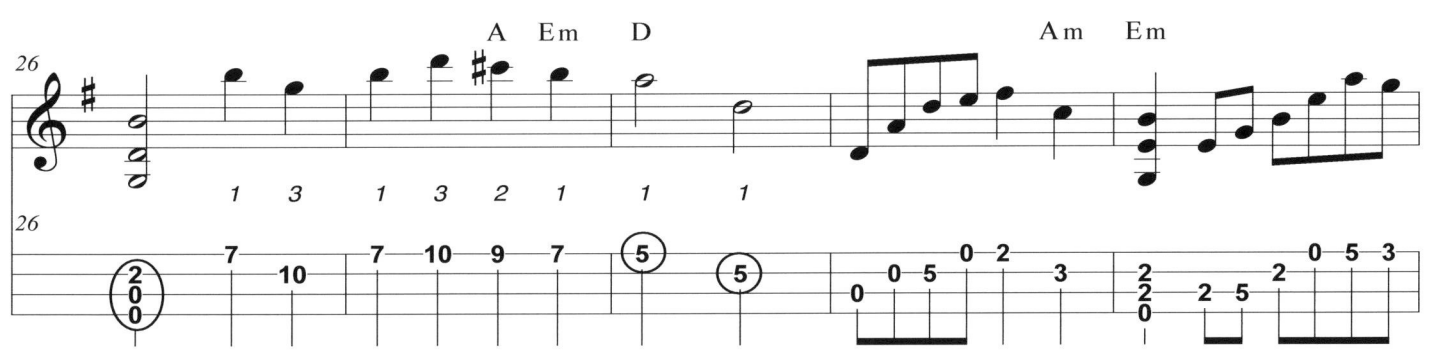
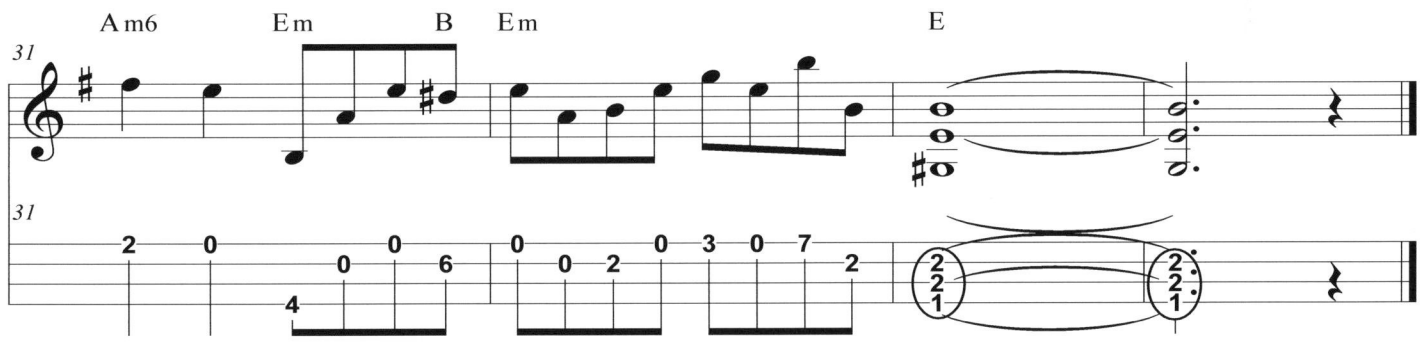

An Italian Rant

John Playford
Arr. by Dix Bruce

Moderato ♩ = 132

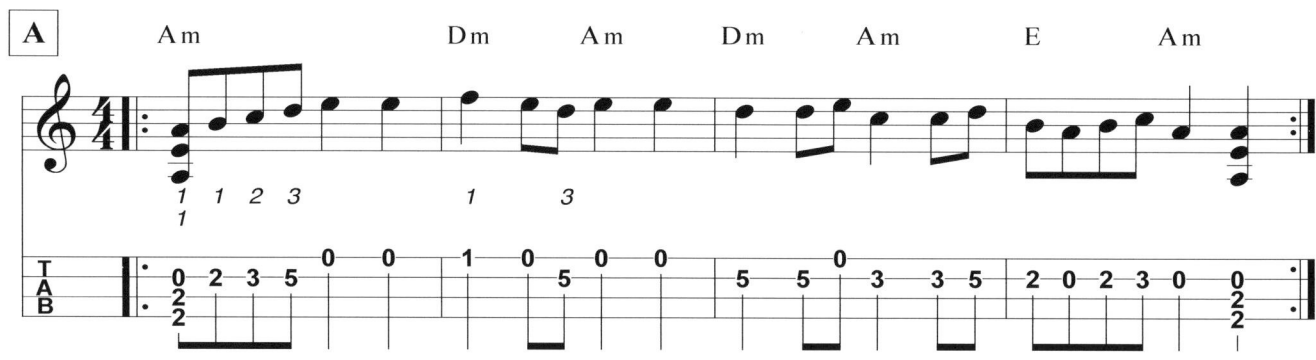

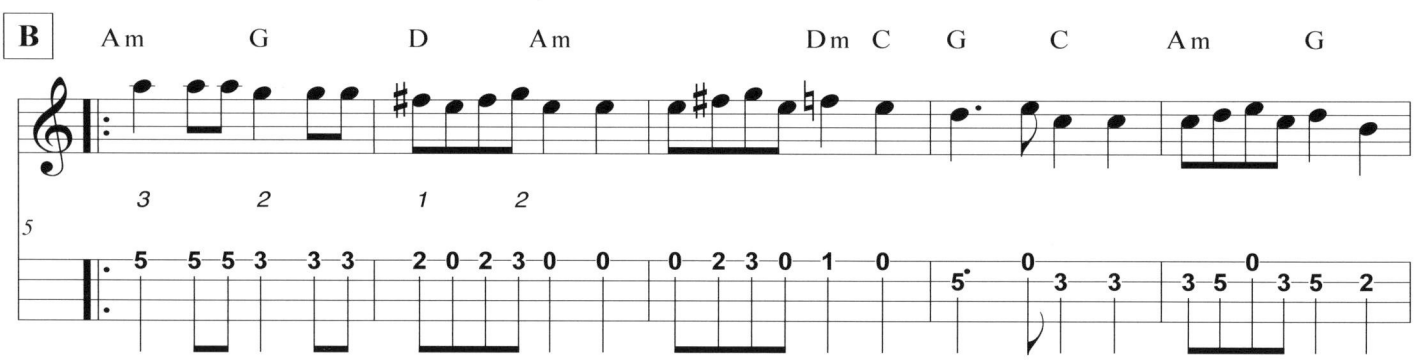

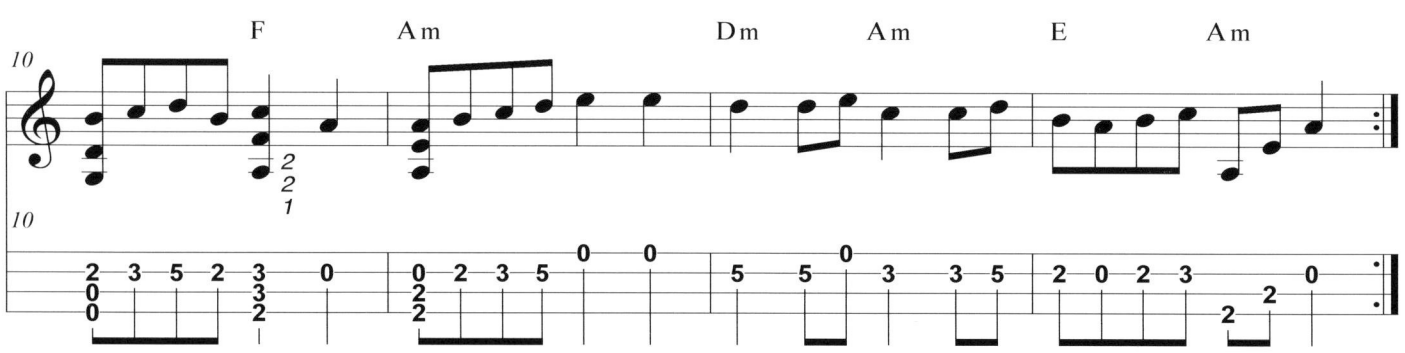

On the Cold Ground

Moderato ♩. = 74

John Playford
Arr. by Dix Bruce

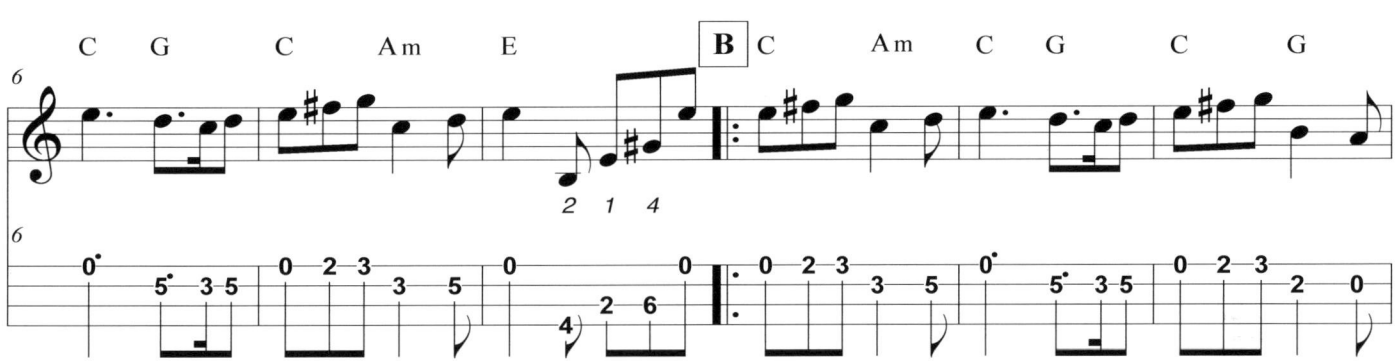

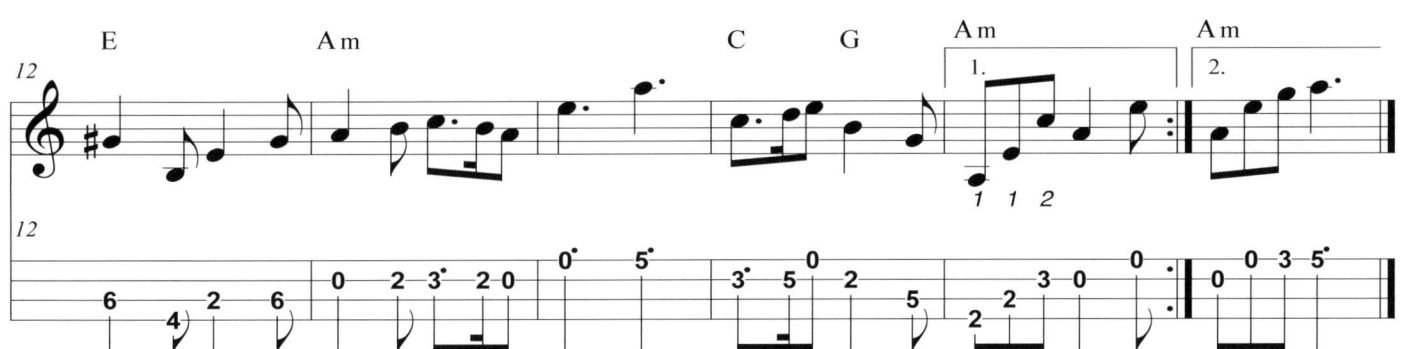

Rendez Á Dieu

Reverently ♩ = 88

Louis Bourgeois 1543
Arr. by Dix Bruce

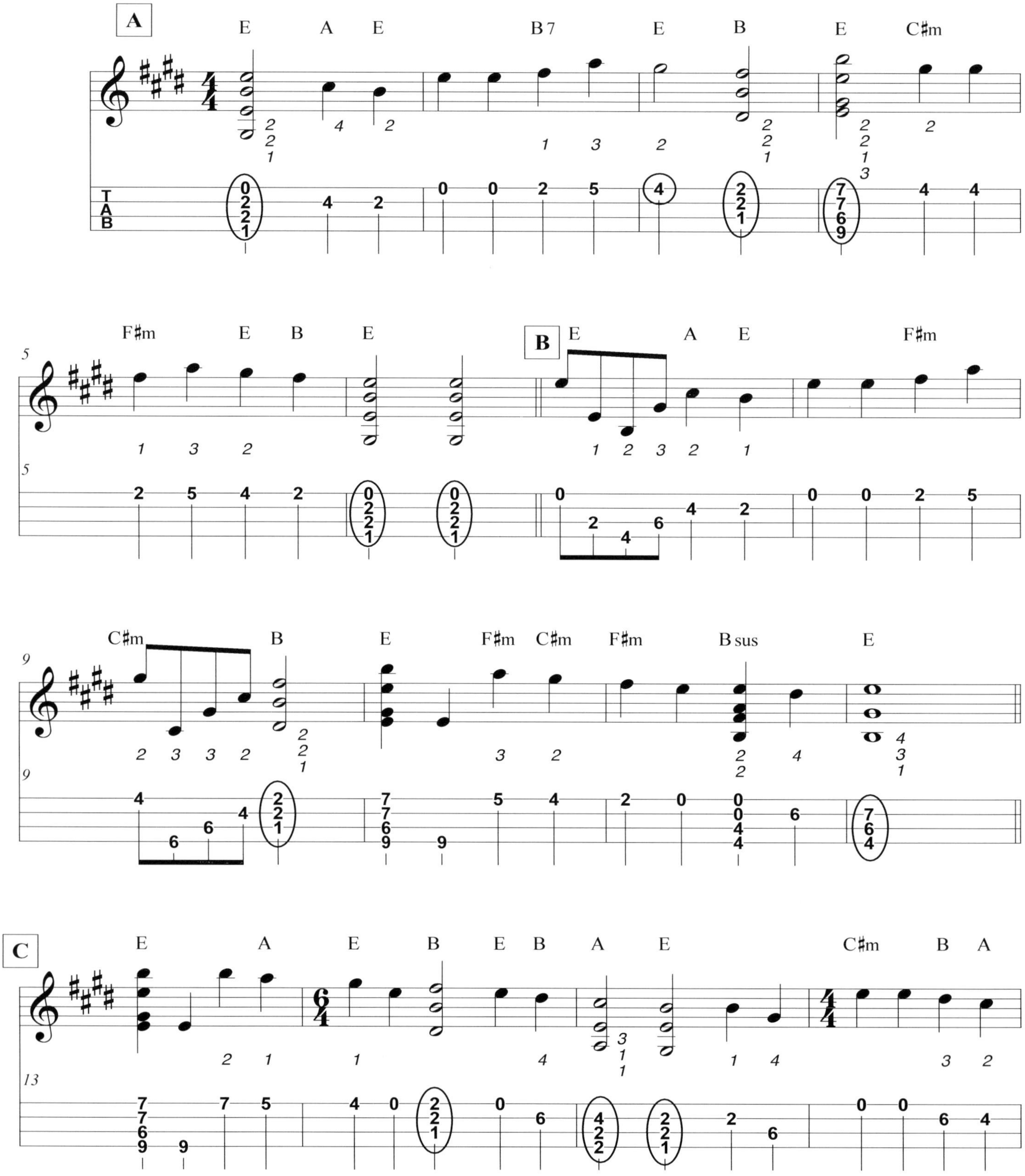

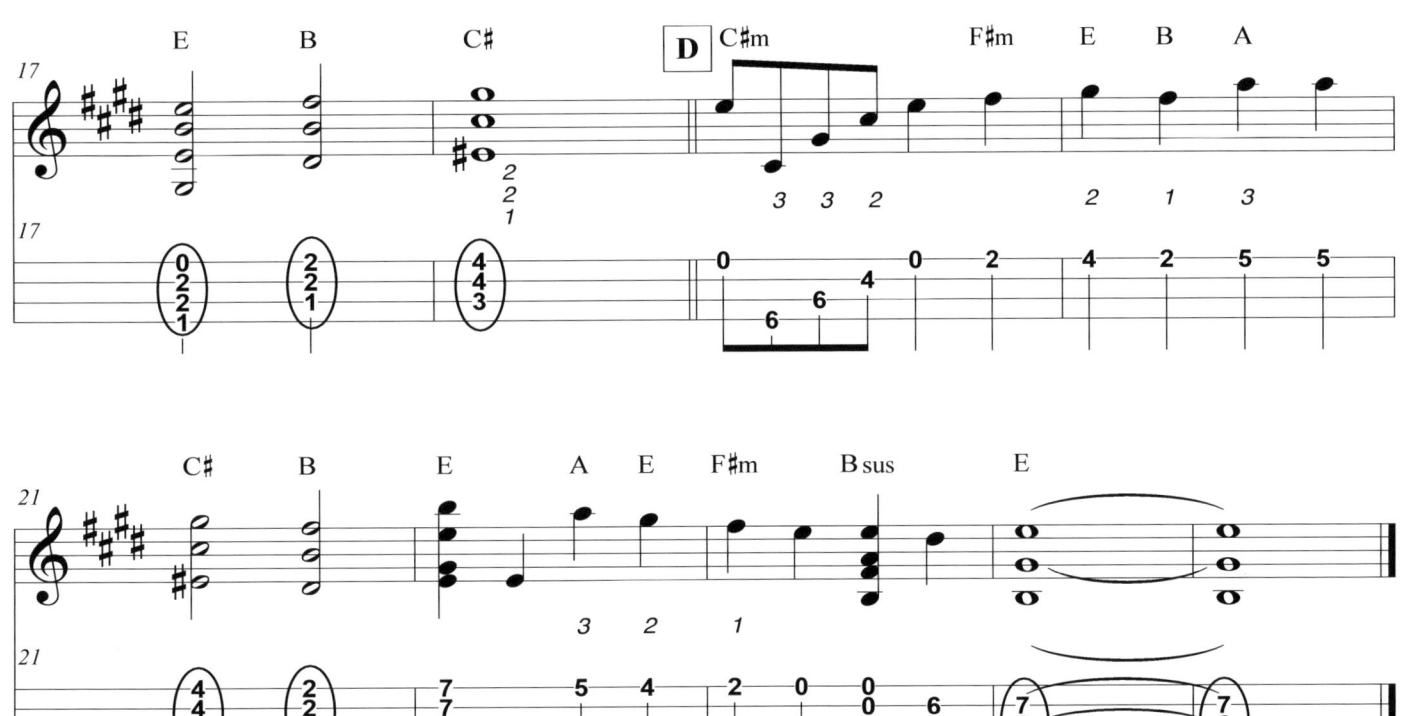

Si Pour t'Aymer

Moderato ♩ = 126

Unknown
Arr. by Dix Bruce

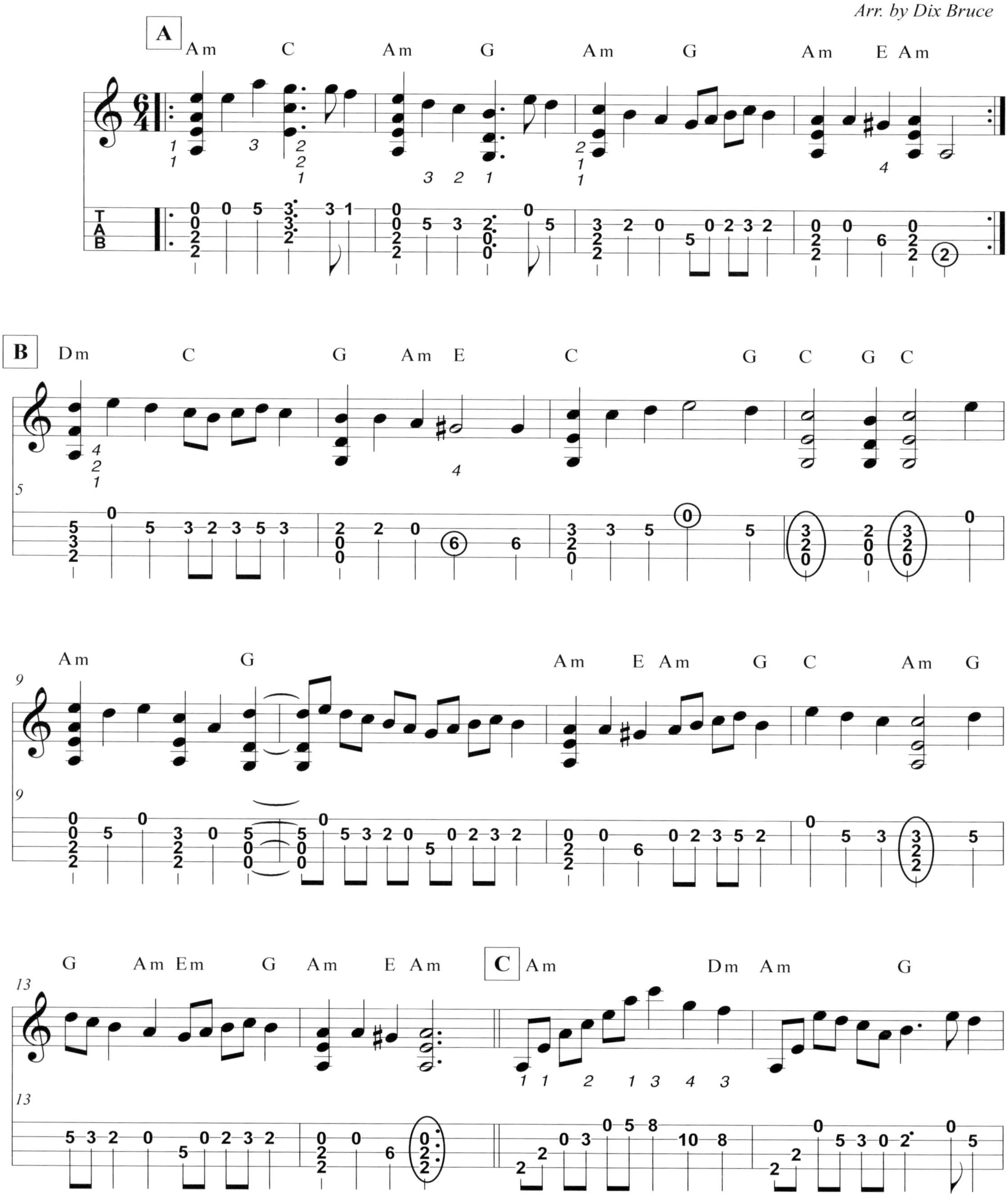

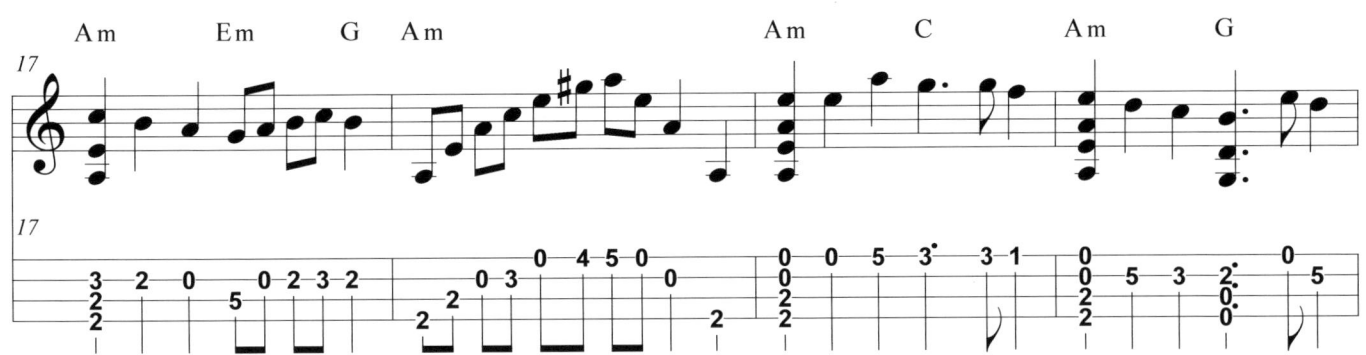
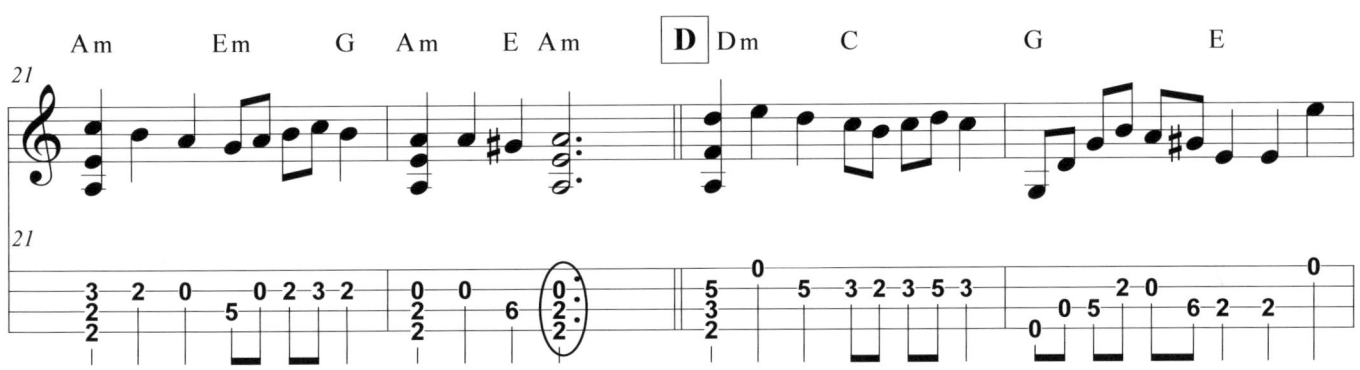
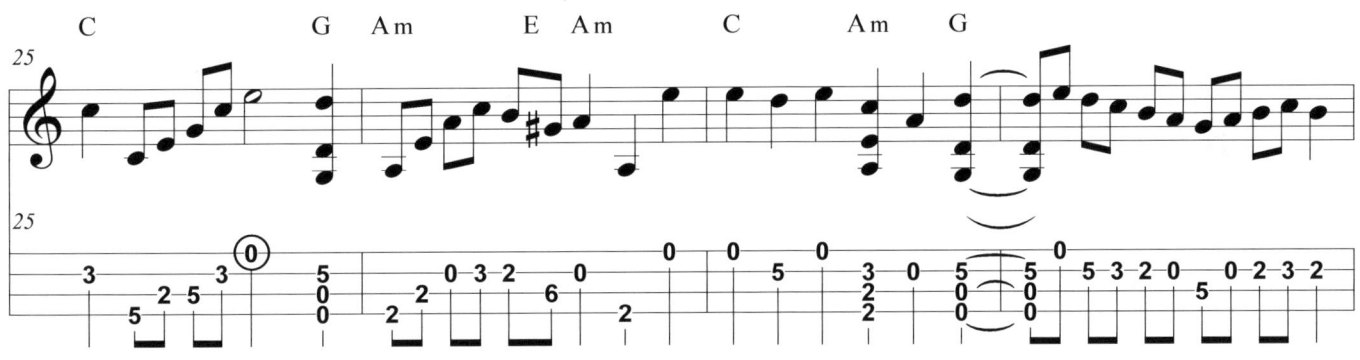
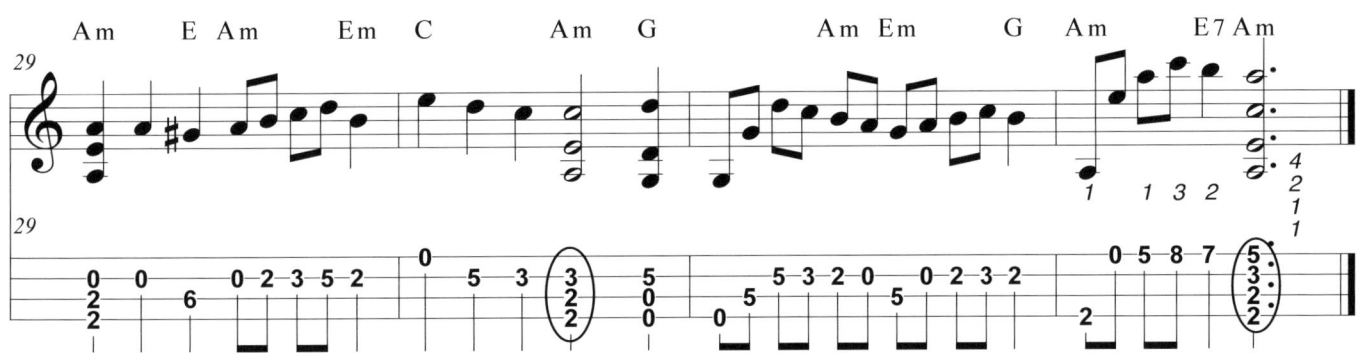

Packington's Pound

Allegro ♩ = 140

Attributed to Francis Cutting late 1600s
Arr. by Dix Bruce

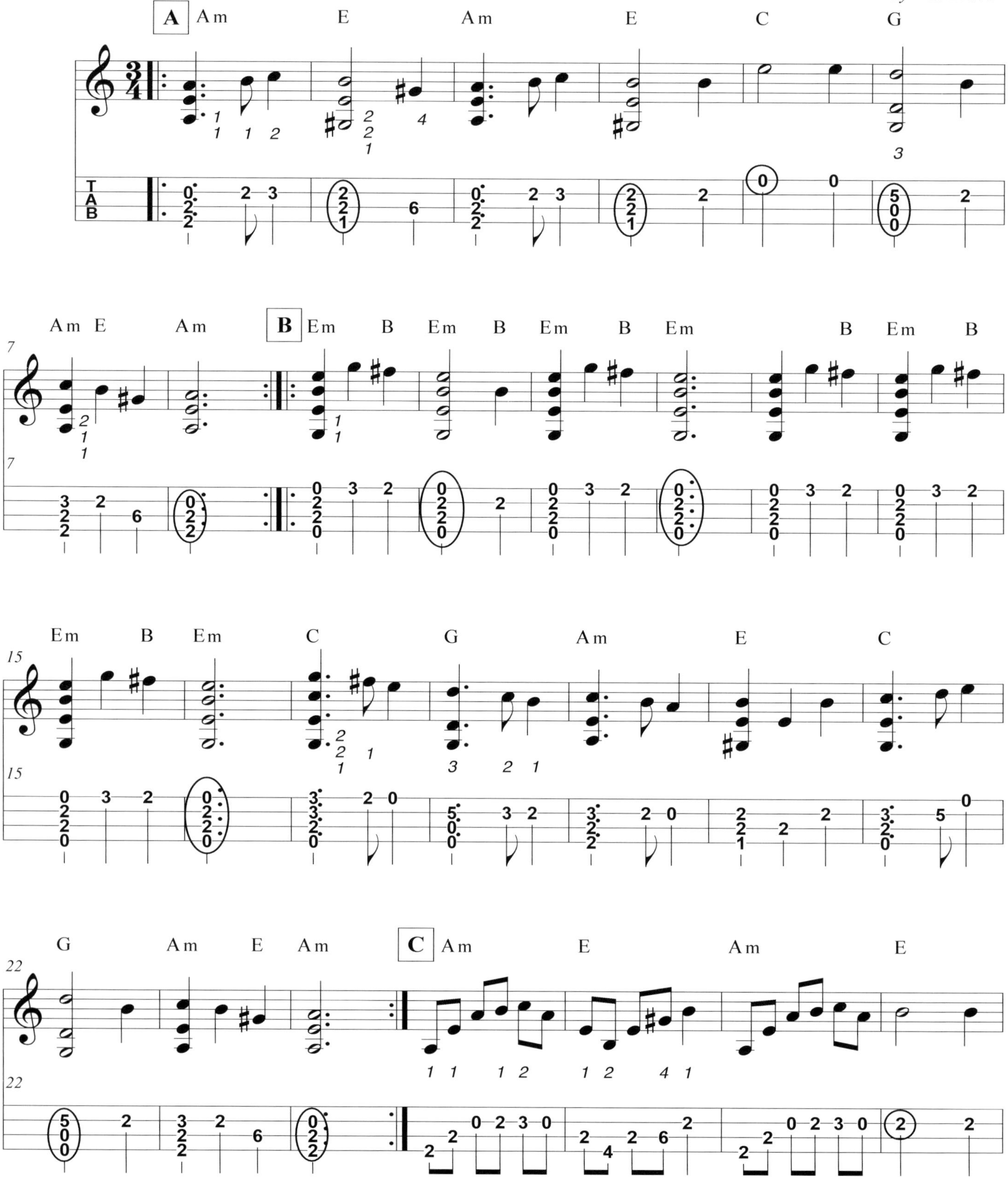

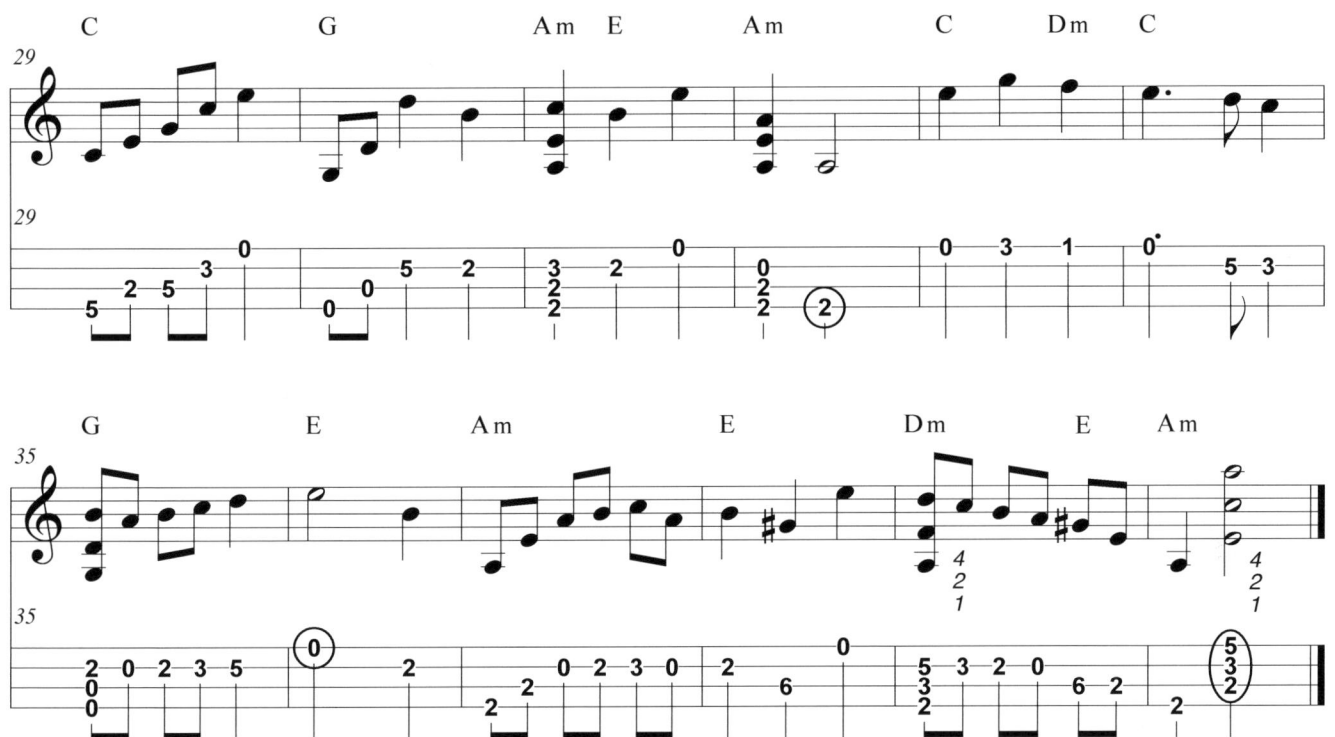

Chestnut

Moderately ♩ = 140

John Playford
Arr. by Dix Bruce

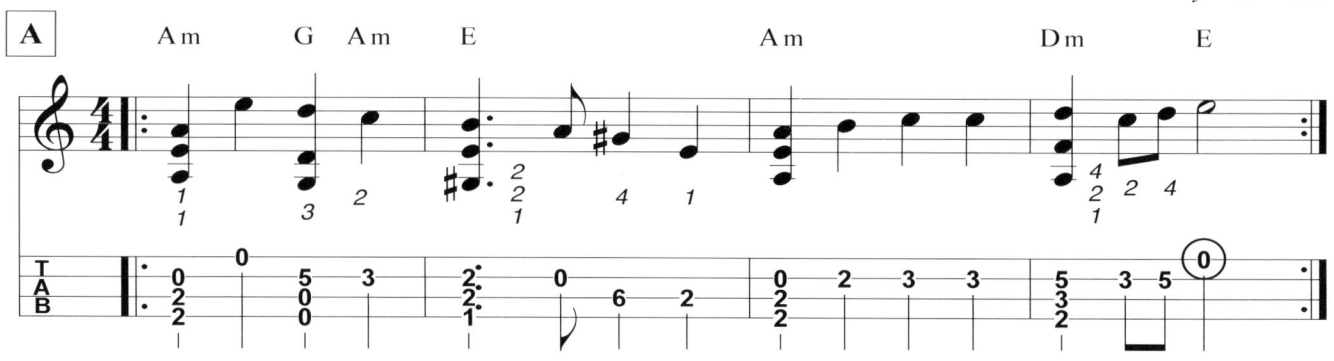

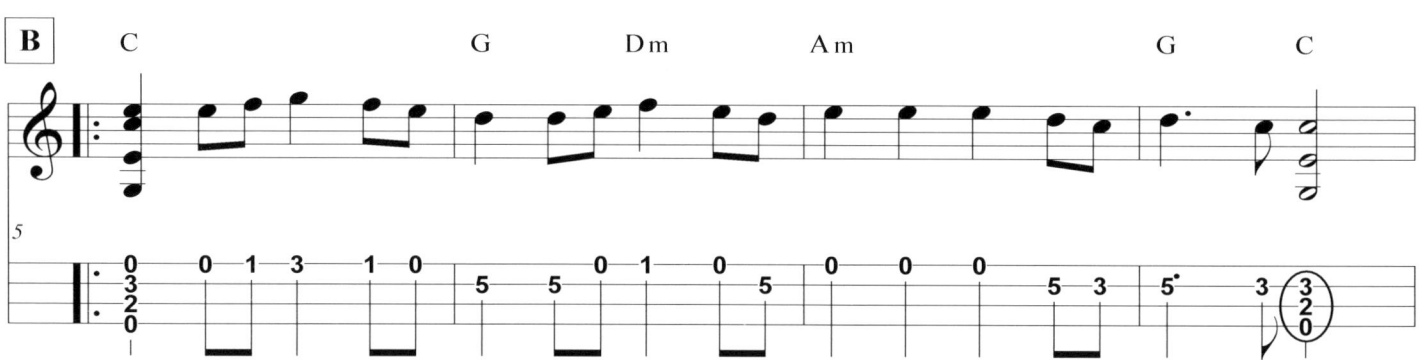

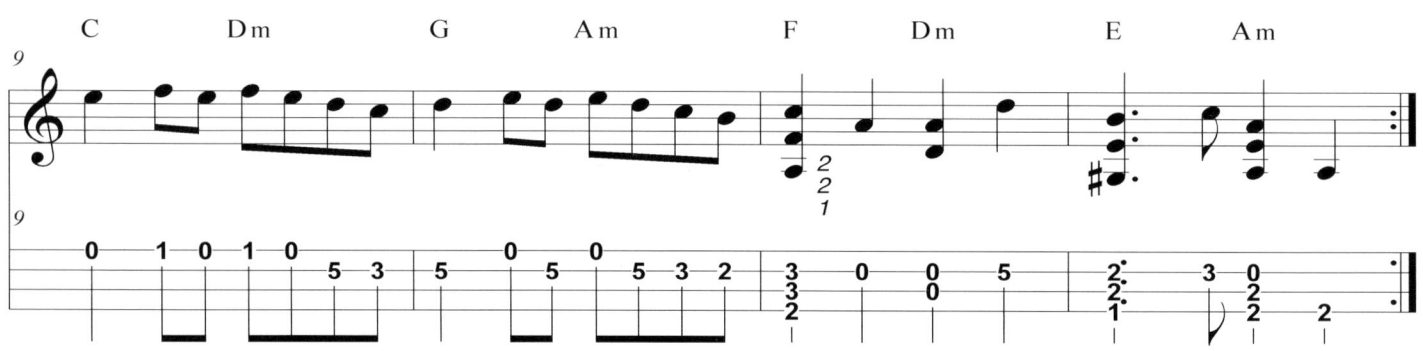

Other Mel Bay Mandolin Books

12 Divertimentos for Solo Mandolin (Oswald/Goodin)
18th Century Mandolin Duets of Jean-Baptiste Miroglio (ed. Barry Trott)
Airs for the Seasons Arranged for Solo Mandolin (Oswald/Goodin)
Bach E Major Prelude from the Partita No. 3 for Solo Violin Transcribed for Mandolin (Driscoll)
Bach's Sonatas and Partitas for Solo Violin Arranged for Mandolin (Driscoll)
Baroque Music for Mandolin (Bancalari)
Baroque Sampler for Octave Mandolin (Goodin)
Cantabile (Baldassari/Mock)
French Baroque Mandolin Suite (Marais/Bancalari)
German Baroque Music for Mandolin (Bancalari)
J. S. Bach for Mandolin (Bancalari)
J. S. Bach Mandolin Duets (Holenko)
J. S. Bach: Two-Part Inventions for Two Mandolins (Bancalari)
Mandolin Classics (Cherednik/Eidson)
Mandolin Classics in Tablature (Bancalari)
Mandolin Instrumentals (Landau)
Playford for Mandolin (Goodin)
Renaissance Solos for Mandolin (Holenko)
Romantic Melodies for Mandolin Solo (Landau)
Telemann for Mandolin (Goodin)
Telemann for Two Mandolins (Goodin)
Tunes from 17th-Century Scotland Arranged for Mandolin (MacKillop)
Vivaldi Concertos for Mandolin (Lemma)
Wedding Music for Mandolin (Bruce)
Wohlfahrt Violin Studies Arranged for Mandolin (Case)
Anthology of Mandolin Music (Orr)
International Favorites for Mandolin (Carr)
Italian Folk Music for Mandolin (LaBarbera)
Mandolin Sampler (Gelo)
Mandolin Songbook (Eidson)
Mandolin Tunes Made Easy: Large Print (W. Bay)
Mandolin Uff Da! Let's Dance: Scandanavian Dance Tunes for Mandolin (Bruce)
Master Anthology of Mandolin Solos Vol. 1 (Multiple Authors)
Northern Italian & Ticino Region Folk Songs for Mandolin (Aonzo/Ponzoni/Borsani)
Traditional Southern Italian Mandolin and Fiddle Music (LaBarbera)
World Music for Mandolin Made Easy (Berthoud)
50 Tunes for Mandolin Vol. 1 (Geslison)
101 Red Hot Bluegrass Mandolin Licks & Solos (McCabe)
All-Time Favorite Parking Lot Picker's Mandolin Solos (Bruce)
Backup Trax/Old-Time & Fiddle Tunes for Fiddle and Mandolin (Bruce)
Blazing Mandolin Solos (Kaufman)

WWW.MELBAY.COM

Other Mel Bay Mandolin Books

Bluegrass Breaks: Mandolin (Bruce)
Chris Thile: Stealing Second
Classic Bluegrass Solos for Mandolin (Collins)
Complete Jethro Burns Mandolin (Burns/Eidson)
Doc and Dawg (Grisman and Watson)
Favorite Mandolin Picking Tunes (Bruce)
Great Mandolin Picking Tunes (Carr)
Kenny Hall's Music Book: Old-Time Music for Fiddle & Mandolin (Hall/Gray)
Lively Mandolin Tunes (Norris)
Monroe Instrumentals: 25 Bill Monroe Favorites (Collins)
New Classics for Bluegrass Mandolin (Baldassari)
Old-Time Mandolin Solos (Eidson/Hayth)
Old-Time Stringband Workshop for Mandolin (Keefer/Weissman/Prohaska)
Old-Time Favorites for Fiddle and Mandolin (Levenson)
Old-Time Festival Tunes for Fiddle and Mandolin (Levenson)
Parking Lot Picker's Play-Along: Mandolin (Bruce)
Parking Lot Picker's Songbook (Bruce)
Shady Grove (Grisman & Garcia)
Southern Mountain Mandolin (Erbsen)
Steve Kaufman's Favorite 50 Mandolin Tunes A-F
Steve Kaufman's Favorite 50 Mandolin Tunes G-M
Steve Kaufman's Favorite 50 Mandolin Tunes N-S
Steve Kaufmans Favorite 50 Mandolin Tunes S-W
String Band Classics for Mandolin (Bruce)
Texas Fiddle Favorites for Mandolin (Carr)
The Mike Marshall Collection
Tone Poems for Mandolin (Grisman)
100 Tunes from O'Neill's Music of Ireland for Mandolin (Allison)
Celtic Mandolin (Driscoll)
Celtic Mandolin Encyclopedia (Bancalari)
Fiddle Tunes & Irish Music for Mandolin (Gelo)
Irish Music for Mandolin Made Easy (Berthoud)
Irish Mandolin Playing: A Complete Guide (Berthoud)
Steve Kaufman's Favorite Celtic Reels for Mandolin
Steve Kaufman's Favorite 50 Celtic Reels for Mandolin
Steve Kaufman's Favorite 50 Jigs and Waltzes for Mandolin
Steve Kaufman's Favorite Celtic Hornpipes for Mandolin
Tunes from 17th-Century Scotland Arranged for Mandolin (MacKillop)
Turlough O'Carolan for Mandolin (Landau)
13 Tango Passions for Mandolin and Guitar (Karasik)
Brazilian Choro: A Method for Mandolin and Bandolim (Mair/Sa)

WWW.MELBAY.COM